THE WISDOM OF THE EAST SERIES

Edited by J. L. CRANMER-BYNG, M.C.

CHINESE BUDDHIST VERSE

Chinese
Buddhist Verse

Translated by
RICHARD ROBINSON

John Murray, Albemarle Street,
London, W.

First Edition . . . 1954

Printed in Great Britain by Butler & Tanner Ltd., Frome and London
and Published by John Murray (Publishers) Ltd.

CONTENTS

	PAGE
Notes on Pronunciation	ix
Introduction	xi
Invocation	xxiv
1. The Acts of the Buddha	1
2. Earnest Faith	13
3. *Equality	16
4. *Ratnakūṭa's Hymn to the Buddha	18
5. *The Bodhisattva's Household	22
6. Parables from the Kāśyapa-parivarta Sūtra	28
7. The Teacher of Religion	31
8. *The Eternal Buddha	33
9. *Universal Mercy	37
10. In Praise of the Buddha	41
11. The Solemn Oath	44
12. *Mercy and the Void	46
13. *In Praise of the Buddha	48
14. The Avataṁsaka Sūtra (selections)	49
15. *Akṣobhya's Land	61
16. The Twelve Verses of Adoration	64
17. The Evening Hymn of Praise	66
18. The Hymn of Right Faith	70
19. The Sūtra of the Sixth Patriarch (selections)	75
20. Faith in Mind	77
Bibliography	82
Notes	83
Index of Chinese Texts Translated	85

Not the traditional title.

DEDICATION

I wish to take this merit and virtue
And turn them over to all everywhere
So that I and other living beings
May all alike achieve full Buddhahood.

EDITORIAL NOTE

The object of the Editor of this series is a very definite one. He desires above all things that these books shall be the ambassadors of good-will between East and West. He hopes that they will contribute to a fuller knowledge of the great cultural heritage of the East, for only through real understanding will the West be able to appreciate the underlying problems and aspirations of Asia to-day. He is confident that a deeper knowledge of the great ideals and lofty philosophy of Eastern thought will help to a revival of that true spirit of charity which neither despises nor fears the nations of another creed and colour.

J. L. CRANMER-BYNG.

50, ALBEMARLE STREET,
LONDON, W.1.

ACKNOWLEDGEMENT

The author wishes to express his grateful acknowledgement to Dr. Edward Conze, who has helped him towards an understanding of things Buddhist, and whose advice has saved this book from a number of errors; and to Dr. Arthur Waley, whose interest in the manuscript has given it the benefit of his great knowledge and experience. Acknowledgement is also due to members of the London Group of the Western Buddhist Order, who showed an interest in these poems as they were being translated.

NOTES ON PRONUNCIATION

This section is merely a rough guide for the convenience of the non-linguist reader whose pleasure may be increased if he knows how to pronounce the names and Oriental terms in a Buddhist text.

Sanskrit

Pronounce : a as in b*u*tter   e   as in fr*e*ight
            ā ,, ,, h*ah*   ai ,, ,, wh*y*
            i ,, ,, p*i*n   o ,, ,, g*o*
            ī ,, ,, mach*i*ne   au ,, ,, h*ow*
            u ,, ,, p*u*t
            ū ,, ,, r*u*de

a, i, and u are short.
ā, ī, ū, e, ai, o, and au are long.

Pronounce : c as ch in *ch*at
            ñ ,, ni ,, o*ni*on
            ś ,, sh ,, *sh*eep
            ṣ ,, sh ,, *sh*eep (approximately).

Indians differentiate ṭ, ḍ, and ṇ from t, d, and n, but in pronunciation Western readers generally ignore the distinction.

Indians pronounce the h in kh, gh, ch, jh, ṭh, ḍh, th, dh, ph, and bh, but for convenience in pronunciation Western readers can ignore this h.

Nowadays Sanskrit is pronounced with a stress accent which falls generally :

On the first of two syllables, e.g. Búddha, Dhárma, Sángha.
On a long second-last syllable, e.g. Abhisambódhi, Nirvā́ṇa.
On the third last syllable when the second last is short, e.g. Tathā́gata, Kā́śyapa, Avatáṁsaka.
On the fourth from the end when two short syllables follow, e.g. Śā́kyamuni, Jétavana, Akṣáyamati.
A syllable is long if it contains ā, ī, ū, ṛ, e, ai, o, or au, or if its vowel

is followed by more than one consonant. (Gh, kh, etc., are single consonants.)

Chinese

Pronounce:
- a as in h*a*h
- e ,, ,, wom*e*n
- i ,, ,, p*i*n mach*i*ne
- o ,, ,, l*aw*
- u ,, ,, r*u*de
- ü ,, ,, German (*Hügel*)
- ch ,, ,, *ye*ah
- erh ,, ,, h*er*
- ih ,, ,, sh*ir*t
- ai ,, ,, wh*y*
- ao as in h*ow*
- ei ,, ,, fr*ei*ght
- ia equals yah
- ieh ,, yeh
- iu ,, yoh
- ou ,, oh
- ua ,, wah
- ui ,, ooey
- uo ,, woh
- üeh ,, weh

Pronounce p, t, k, ch, and ts as b, d, g, j, and dz.
Pronounce p', t', k', ch', and ts' as p, t, k, ch, and ts.
Hs has approximately the sound of sh in *sh*eep.
Tzu is pronounced dzzz, with buzzing of the z's instead of a vowel.

INTRODUCTION

This book is intended to document a spiritual movement in terms of the hymns it has produced. The Chinese Buddhist Canon is, to use one of its own similes, like the great ocean. It abounds in rare gems as well as strange monsters, and it conserves many diverse deposits which the streams of history have carried into it. It preserves the traces of successive religious impulses which arose in India and radiated through areas of influence in South-East Asia, Central Asia, and the Far East, and which disappeared from India, leaving few documents there. It stores a large literature, both exegetical and original, that was produced during the centuries in which Buddhism took root and matured in China. In this ocean of literature, among the remains of dead cults and philosophies, there are a number of scriptures which are read, believed and followed to-day, and whose influence is likely to persist. These are either the basic texts of organized sects or are enduring favourites with all sects. Most of the hymns in this book have been selected from these living scriptures.

Chinese Buddhist 'gāthās' are written in blank verse with four, five or seven characters to a line. They are usually divisible into quatrains, though groups of six or eight lines also occur. As this verse is unrhymed, it does not count as 'shih' or poetry in the narrow sense. However, this form proved a good one for rendering Sanskrit verse, and it translates into English with less loss than other kinds of Chinese verse.

With two or three exceptions, each line of English in this book corresponds to a single line of the Chinese, and each English line contains eight, ten or fourteen syllables, depending on whether the Chinese line consists of four, five or seven characters. I have not used any consistent metrical system, nor have I attempted to reproduce the rhyme of the Chinese in selections 19 and 20.

Though some of the 'gāthās' are in beautiful Chinese, it would be a mistake to judge these hymns by the standards of secular poetry. Being collective literature, like epics and folk-songs, they are concerned more with affirming and enhancing a group's doctrines and attitudes than with individual expression. They use stock themes and stereotyped images. Their authorship is frequently anonymous. They are meant to be chanted in ritual or recited before the assemblies of monks, nuns, laymen and laywomen. Hence they employ many of the same techniques as modern advertising—the use of slogans, repetition, vivid sense-appeal, exaggeration, suggestion, and metaphors heavily charged with familiar associations. In short, they are propaganda.

The inertness of modern Buddhism has provided a basis for the notion that Buddhism is not a proselytizing religion. However, as their verses testify, the Buddhists of eighteen hundred years ago were ardent evangelists. Wandering preachers ranged throughout the Indian and Far Eastern worlds, reciting the scriptures, translating, and bringing the Good Law to the greatest possible number of living beings. *The Teacher of Religion* indicates that there were martyrs among these missionaries. The same poem exhibits the curious doubleness of the preacher's life. He practises meditation in the solitude of the wilderness, and yet is moved by compassion to go out and preach to the four assemblies and to face hostile mobs.

Akṣobhya's Land, which is the 'commercial' of some itinerant text-reciter, shows that the preachers' appeal was directed to the lay public who supported them with alms and assistance. In Buddhist literature, the layman is most frequently a merchant, which is quite appropriate as the merchant community seems to have been the main support of the Order. Preachers travelled under protection of merchant caravans and built their shrines along the trade routes where travelling salesmen could deposit their alms and store up credit in heaven. Praises of the good king occur in Buddhist hymns, and subversive ideas are exceedingly rare, which facts are related to the Order's dependence on royal donors, from whom it received land, buildings, endowments of villages, and exemption from taxation and conscription.

In most countries the monastic community has been the backbone of Buddhism. It provides leisure and security, with facilities for leading the religious life, such as teachers, halls, libraries, shrines and images. It is a refuge for the delicate and the shiftless. It has been an asylum for the sick and insane, who otherwise would have had no one to care for them. It is a retreat for retired generals, politicians and businessmen who want to spend their last years in spiritual cultivation. In ages when monasteries took the place that universities hold nowadays, it was also a stepping-stone to success for philosophers and poets. And not least, it is a stable gathering-place for the lay people who accept the faith and in return give their alms and their younger sons and daughters to the monasteries.

The lay community has always been the flesh and blood of Buddhism, though the dignity of the lay life has fluctuated widely with time and place. In the phase represented by the *Dharmapada*, the layman's chief duty was to give alms to the monks, so that he might go to heaven, and eventually gain a fortunate rebirth and become a monk. In the phase represented by the *Vimalakīrti Sūtra*, the householder saint was exalted above the monks. Here spirituality and monasticism ceased to be synonymous. In the Pure Land sects, the faith of a layman is as good as the faith of a monk. Acts other than the offering of gratitude to Amida are reliance on self-power and inimical to faith. As monasticism encourages this self-pride, it was abandoned by the founder of Jōdoshinshū, and plays a minor part in Jōdoshū. Zen seems to have begun as a popular movement bringing the religion of insight to laymen and under-privileged monks who had had access to nothing higher than the religion of good works and merit. In China and Japan it has always been popular with educated and well-to-do laymen.

The interests of this world have always been an important part of Buddhism, as of other religions. Eighteen centuries ago, the hazards of life were far greater than to-day. Food supply and distribution were precarious, and famines were frequent. Plague and disease ravaged uncontrolled. Robbers operated everywhere and policing was non-existent. Kings were arbitrary, and the law was a menace rather than a protection. Unlimited families were a form of social security, but they were also a terrible fetter on individual freedom. Thus it is natural that monks extolled the blessings of a life free from families and economic concerns, and that householders sought the aid of religion in coping with the perils of existence. *Universal Mercy* is an example of the intense wishful thinking which they pitted against uncontrollable circumstances.

Certain general notions run throughout all the phases of Buddhism represented in this book. Among them are those of ancient Indian cosmology, according to which the frame of the world-structure is three planes (dhātus) stacked one above the other. First is the plane of desire (kāmadhātu), which contains the paths of hell, hungry ghosts, animals and men. Second is the plane of form (rūpadhātu), which is stratified into seventeen heavens. Third is the plane of formlessness, which contains four heavens. Mount Sumeru goes up through the centre of the desire-plane and form-plane, which are surrounded by a ring of iron mountains. There are six main grades of being or ' destinies '—inhabitants of hell, hungry ghosts, animals, men, demons and gods—which are fixed ranks to which beings ascend or descend with variations in their spiritual specific gravity. These destinies and their subdivisions occupy various layers within the three planes. Only men can attain Nirvāṇa, or birth in a paradise where Nirvāṇa is attainable. Even the gods have to leave their heavenly mansions when their stock of merit is spent.

Transitions from one destiny to another occur after death. The individual stream of dispositions, with its merit and demerit, flows from one birth to another, and so on through the round of cosmic flux (saṁsāra) until liberation is achieved.

All existence in the three planes is suffering, because it is contaminated by the passions—lust, hatred, ignorance, pride, wrong view, etc. The object of the religious life is purification from the passions and realization of enlightenment (bodhi) which shines through when the clouds of impurity are dispersed. It is the transcendental Other Shore, beyond the river of cosmic flux. This state is uncontaminated, good, happy and immutable, but it is also inconceivable and indescribable. It is said to be the same as cosmic flux when seen from an enlightened point of view.

The Way to Enlightenment is training in morality, meditation and wisdom. Through keeping the precepts of morality, merit is accumulated and the passions are weakened. Through meditation and wisdom, wrong views and the passions are overcome, and the sun of insight is allowed to shine. This threefold training is analysed further into enumerations such as the Six Perfections, the Eightfold Path, and the Thirty-Seven Wings of Enlightenment.

All except the first three poems are Mahāyāna. That is, they deal with the course of the bodhisattva, the enlightenment-being or hero of enlightenment, whose way is contrasted with that of the śrāvakas (mere hearers, disciples), and the pratyeka-buddhas (private buddhas, or solitary wise men). The śrāvakas were equated with the Hīnayāna sects (Sarvāstivādins, Sautrāntikas, Theravādists, etc.), which was unkind to these sects and not quite factual. There is a polemical vein running through Mahāyāna literature, and some streaks of it appear in these gāthās.

When a being has accumulated some roots of goodness, has met a good counsellor, and has heard the doctrine, he is able to put forth the thought of supreme enlightenment and become a bodhisattva. He resolves to attain enlightenment for his own sake and for that of all living beings. He makes vows specifying what he will do to benefit beings. Then he cultivates the Perfections and ascends a series of ten stages (bhūmis) till he is equal in every way to a full Buddha. But he does not enter extinction and abandon living beings in the three planes. Because of the vows he made when he first put forth the thought of enlightenment, he remains in the world and works for universal liberation.

Every bodhisattva, when he becomes a Buddha, sets up a Pure Land, a region which he presides over and which serves as a hot-house for growing the seeds of enlightenment. It is one of the devices or good means (upāya) which a bodhisattva masters during the last stages of his training. Conditions for admission vary from land to land. Good works will ensure entry into Akṣobhya's Land. Faith alone is the passport to Amitābha's Land. The furnishings of a Pure Land are designed to attract people whose love of glitter is at present stronger than their love of metaphysics. The jewels, trees, ponds, etc., are taken symbolically by the commentators, which seems legitimate enough as the images used are widespread and natural symbols.

The bodhisattva's world-view differs from the śrāvaka's. He looks at things from a transcendental point of view, while the śrāvaka sees things from a common point of view. Seen transcendentally, all the elements of experience (dharmas) neither arise nor perish, are neither real nor unreal, are void of self and substance. They are just as they are, which is termed their 'suchness' (tathatā). Nevertheless, the bodhisattva continues to play the game of the common world, for the sake of beings who have not yet grown out of it. He participates in the changes going on in an empty world, and does countless good deeds to benefit its inhabitants.

The Buddha in the bodhisattva-yāna is at once the ground of true being (Essence Body, Dharmakāya), the glorified superman identical with true being (Enjoyment Body, Sambhogakāya), and the manifestation of truth in human form (Created Body, Nirmāṇakāya). Buddhahood means a state of perfect wisdom, compassion and good means. From the phenomenal point of view there seem to be countless Buddhas, but in the transcendental realm, Buddhahood is beyond duality and plurality. All the Buddhas give off an effulgence of wisdom and compassion which shines on all living beings, enlivening the seeds of enlightenment and sustaining the bodhisattvas in their course.

Though most of the selections in this book are Mahāyāna, and though the Mahāyāna influence is predominant in modern Chinese and Japanese Buddhism, it should be mentioned here that the Chinese Canon contains the Hīnayāna Sūtra-Pitaka in various versions, as well as the Vinayas and Abhidharmas of several Hīnayāna sects. Furthermore, much error and bad feeling could be avoided if it were realized that the terms 'Hīnayāna' and 'Mahāyāna' are empty of any self-nature. Value-judgments and total contrasts between Hīnayāna and Mahāyāna almost always go astray because there are so many forms of each, and because most of the doctrines considered characteristically Mahāyāna are found in some Hīnayāna sect or other, while the Mahāyānists did not abandon their Hīnayāna heritage. Moreover, all the Indian sects developed and influenced each other, and all were influenced by the non-Buddhists around them.

Though this anthology by no means represents the entire gamut of Buddhist literature, something ought to be said about the affinities of the selections included in it, as they do typify classes of scriptural writing.

One important body of Buddhist literature deals with lives of the Buddha. Most of the material in these is legend, which does not detract from their literary and religious value. The figure of the Buddha has been a glowing ideal towards which Buddhists have directed faith, adoration and aspiration. Thus it is not surprising that epics have been written about this hero who, unlike the heroes of many other epics, excelled in gentleness and wisdom. To represent this genre, I have chosen selections from Aśvaghoṣa's *Buddhacarita*.

Every religion has its collections of maxims. In Buddhism, the need for moral uplift is met principally by the *Dharmapada*. It has passed through various recensions, of which there survive the Pāli *Dhammapada*, in twenty-six chapters, the Tibetan *Udānavarga*, in thirty-nine chapters, and the Chinese *Fa-Chü-Ching*, in thirty-nine chapters. The book, in spite of the limitations usual to collections of maxims, is animated by an ethical earnestness and hermit calm which account for its enduring popularity.

Buddhism possesses an extensive literature of edifying tales. Often they read like folk-tales with moralizing superimposed. The verses on *Equality* in this anthology, taken from such a collection, indicate that anciently, as to-day, this literature was directed to the common people.

A significant class of sūtras deals with the bodhisattva-yāna. These are usually short texts, with some central theme, such as non-duality in the *Vimalakīrti-Nirdeśa*, praising the bodhisattva who has just awakened the thought of enlightenment and providing him with lively, useful advice for his course to perfection. It has been impossible to give an adequate selection from these texts, as they show great originality and diversity. The *Kāśyapaparivarta* is a sūtra of this kind.

Other sūtras recount the power and glory of some Buddha or superhuman bodhisattva, and enjoin faith in him. These texts vary considerably in content and spirit, but share the theme of salvation through devotion. The *Saddharma-Puṇḍarīka* preaches an eternal Śākyamuni. The *Sukhāvatī-Vyūha* tells the history and describes the paradise of the Buddha Amitābha.

There are also sūtras which are ' philosophers' notebooks ', in which doctrine is predominant and in which edification and devotion are subordinate. The selection from the *Laṅkāvatāra* shows these two aspects—wisdom and compassion—fused together.

One sūtra, the *Avataṁsaka*, defies brief description, because it is really a whole family of sūtras, of varying ages, styles and contents. It contains two texts, the *Daśabhūmika* and the *Gandavyūha*, which are well known as separate works.

Buddhism seems to have come to China along the Central Asian trade routes about A.D. 60. The *Later Han History* states that in A.D. 66, Ying, prince of Ch'u, had Buddhist rites carried out. It is also reported that, a year before this, Emperor Ming dreamt about a giant golden man. He sent a mission to the Western Countries which is said to have returned with images, books and two translators. There are also indications that Buddhism came by sea to South China at an early date. However, it was two centuries before it really took hold in China, though missionaries came from time to time and left translations and tiny groups of students.

From A.D. 222 to A.D. 265 China was divided into three warring states which ravaged and depopulated the country with their campaigns. In 224, at the beginning of this time of trouble, two Indians, Wei-chih-nan and Chu Lü-yen, arrived in Wuchang, where they translated the *Dharmapada*. Then about A.D. 250 there arrived in Loyang, capital of Wei, the northern one of the three states, a Sogdian missionary named Saṅghavarman, to whom the most popular version of the *Sukhāvatī-Vyūha* is attributed.

By A.D. 401, when the great translator Kumārajīva arrived in Ch'ang-an, the monastic system was firmly established, and Buddhist cult practices were widespread among the people. A good number of sūtras had been translated, but the phrasing was clumsy and the terminology was inexact. With the help of his Chinese scribes and students, Kumārajīva retranslated most of the popular texts, as well as a number of philosophical treatises which had not been known in China previously.

Translations were generally made by teams, headed by an Indian or Central Asian missionary who held the Sanskrit text and read it out, rendering it sentence by sentence into Chinese, often with the help of an interpreter. The translation was written down by a Chinese assistant who 'held the brush'. In the better-organized teams, Chinese who knew Sanskrit checked on the meaning and discussed obscure points with the translator who 'held the text'. The phrasing of the translations was generally checked by a Chinese stylist. The foreign missionaries spoke Chinese with varying degrees of proficiency, but do not seem to have read or written it. Kumārajīva, who had spoken Chinese for twenty years before beginning his work of translation, seems to have thoroughly mastered the spoken language.

As Buddhism took hold in China, it spread beyond the little circles of missionaries' disciples and became the religion of the people. The Amitābha cult was in vogue at least as early as A.D. 390 when Hui-Yüan, a gentleman-monk with eclectic views, founded the White Lotus Society on Mount Lu, in Hunan. He and his disciples had moments of fervour, but they also followed other practices and their adherence to the Pure Land was only partial.

T'an-luan (Japanese 'Donran') was first a student of the sūtras. Then he fell sick and took to Taoism in a search for health and long life. He met the Indian missionary Bodhiruci, who taught him that the true longevity is in enlightenment, and instructed him in meditation on the Buddha Amitāyus. He burned his Taoist books and thereafter devoted himself exclusively to Amidism. He died in A.D. 542, at the age of sixty-seven. (See *Hymn of Right Faith*.)

Tao-ch'o (Dōshaku) left the household life at the age of fourteen. He studied the Mahāparinirvāṇa Sūtra for a while. Then he read T'an-luan's epitaph and was greatly moved. He gave up the Nirvāṇa Sūtra and concentrated on calling Amida's name. Thereafter he lectured more than two hundred times on the Amitāyur-dhyāna Sūtra and instructed both monks and laity until his death in A.D. 645.

Shan-tao (Zendō) heard Tao-ch'o lecturing on the Amitāyur-dhyāna Sūtra and his heart awakened to entire faith in the calling of Amida's name. He preached often to monks and laymen in the capital, exhorting them to seek rebirth in Amida's paradise. He wrote out the *Smaller Sukhāvatī-Vyūha Sūtra* more than a hundred thousand times, and painted many pictures of the Pure Land. When he recited the name of Amida, a radiant splendour proceeded from his mouth. (See *Hymn of Right Faith*, the third line under 'Zendō'.) He wrote a number of treatises which laid the basis for modern Pure Land teachings, and compiled a liturgy for daily use, *The Praises of Rebirth*, which is still popular. He died in A.D. 681.

In Japan, Zendō's books inspired Hōnen (A.D. 1133–1212), who became the founder of the Jōdoshū (Pure Land Sect). Like other earnest people of his time, he had become dissatisfied with the sordid politics and sterile scholarism of the great monasteries, and when he broke the trail, multitudes followed him in the way of simple devotion. Among them was a young man named Shinran (A.D. 1173–1262), around whom there grew up a sect now known as Jōdoshinshū, which is the largest in present-day Japan.

During the fifth and sixth centuries, while some Chinese monks were lecturing in the monasteries and developing vast doctrinal systems, others were out in little hermitages among the hills, meditating and sustaining their efforts by reading some text such as the Laṅkāvatāra or the Vajracchedika. Bodhidharma, reputedly the first patriarch of Zen in China, seems to have been one of these mountain meditation masters. The tradition says that Bodhidharma transmitted his doctrine, together with his robe, to Hui-k'o, who passed both to Seng-ts'an, the third patriarch, who is the reputed author of *Faith in Mind*. The sixth patriarch, Hui-neng, transmitted his doctrine to a number of disciples, but did not transmit the robe. From this time, Zen came out of obscurity. Its followers became numerous and acquired monasteries of their own. It is most likely that the sayings of Hui-neng were compiled into a scripture by followers of Shen-hui (A.D. 668–760), who has been called the seventh patriarch. This scripture has remained popular in China until the present day, and, in English and French translation, has a wide vogue among Western Buddhists.

A Mahāyāna sūtra usually contains a paragraph assuring merit more incalculable than the sands of the Ganges to whoever recites, chants, reads, accepts, retains and propagates even four lines of it. Whether or not readers of this book are interested in the merit which they may accumulate thereby, they will undoubtedly find the greatest satisfaction if they read Buddhist scriptures as their authors intended them to be read. Study and analysis would stultify, whereas frequent, fluent reading and re-reading make the undertones of feeling more vivid and intense. Furthermore, the reading of scriptures is intended to be a religious act, and as such requires its own kind of participation from the reader. The appreciation of Buddhism calls for a detached sympathy, which was what Seng-ts'an had in mind when he said:

> "If you would see it before you,
> Do not concur, do not object.
> Let it go, and it is itself;
> Its essence neither goes nor stays."

INVOCATION

I GO for refuge to the *Honoured Ones*,
Who everywhere confer great benefits,
Whose boundless wisdom is self-dependent,
Who save and guard all in the ten quarters;
And to that sea of essence and features,
The *Doctrine*, whose words and sense are 'no-self';
And that endless virtue-store, the *Order*
Of those who strive for full enlightenment.

1. THE ACTS OF THE BUDDHA

Aśvaghoṣa's *Buddhacarita*

Translated into Chinese by Dharmakṣema, between A.D. 414 and 421

The great Buddhist poet Aśvaghoṣa is believed to have lived during the first half of the first century A.D. His native country was probably in East India, and it is likely that he belonged to a branch of the Mahāsaṅghikas, a sect from which the Mahāyāna emerged. He was quite learned in non-Buddhist knowledge, and is said to have been converted from Brahmanism. His poetical works were designed to present the essentials of the Buddhist faith in clear and glowing terms. The *Buddhacarita* holds a high place in Sanskrit literature, though unfortunately chapters fourteen to twenty-eight survive only in Chinese and Tibetan translation.

Chapter One : Birth

There was a scion of the Ikṣvāku
An invincible king of the Śākyas,
Who was called by the name Śuddhodana
Because he was pure in wealth and virtue.
The multitudes looked up to him gladly
Even as they looked up to the new moon.
The king was like Śakra, lord of the gods;
His queen was like Śacī, queen of the gods.
Her firm purpose was steady as the earth;
Her heart was pure as a lotus blossom.
In similitude she was named Māyā,[1]
Though really she was incomparable.
A divine lord of elephants came down
On her in spirit to dwell in her womb.

A mother, though free from grief and distress,
She had no deceptive, false ideas.
Being sick of the world's noisy clamour,
She longed to be in a secluded grove,
The excellent garden of Lumbinī,
Where springs trickled and flowers and fruit were lush.
Tranquil and disposed to meditation,
She asked the king's permission to go there.
The king, understanding her intention,
Was seized by a strange and special concern.
He commanded his entire retinue
To proceed to the grove in that garden.
At that time the sovereign lady Māyā
Knew that her time to give birth had arrived.
She lay at ease on a most restful couch,
Attended by a hundred thousand maids.
The time was the fourth month and the eighth day.
The weather was suitably clear and mild.
While she fasted and observed pure conduct,
Bodhisattva was born from her right side,
Out of compassion to save the world,
Without making his mother suffer pain.
As King Aurva came to birth from the thigh,
As King Prithu came to birth from the hand,
As King Māndhātri was born from the head,
As Kakshīvat was born from the armpit,
In a like manner the bodhisattva
Came out into the world through the right side.
His splendour shone brilliantly all around
As bit by bit he emerged from the womb;
Just as if he had descended from space,
He did not proceed through the gates of life.
Having stored virtue through countless ages

He knew that he was born to deathlessness.
Calmly, attentively and not stumbling,
He came forth, wondrously grave and sedate.
In radiance he appeared from the womb,
Just like the sun when it first arises.
Men looked at his extremely bright splendour
And yet it did not injure their eyes.
They loosed their gaze without being dazzled,
As if looking at the moon in the sky.
The rays from his body shone brilliantly,
Like the sun which eclipses the lanterns.
The bodhisattva's true golden body
Shone everywhere even in this manner.
Upright, firm and undisturbed in mind,
Tranquil and poised, he took seven paces.
The soles of his feet, with their straight insteps,
Left prints that glittered like the seven stars.
He strode like the lion, the king of beasts;
He looked around in the four directions;
He penetrated the ultimate truth
And with majesty spoke in this manner:
  " This birth is the birth of a Buddha!
    It is the last boundary of birth!
    In the course of this one last life
    I am to liberate everyone!"
Straightway from the middle of the heavens
There descended two streams of pure water,—
One which was warm, one which was cold and fresh,—
To baptize his head and soothe his body.
He resided in a jewelled palace
And lay on a lapis-lazuli couch.
The kings of the gods, golden flowers in hand,
Held up the four feet of the bed.

All the gods in the middle of the sky
Attended him with jewelled canopies.
They sensed his grandeur and sang his praises,
Exhorting him to become a Buddha.
All the dragon-kings were glad and rejoiced,
And longed ardently for the supreme Law.
Having already served former Buddhas,
They now got to meet the bodhisattva.
They scattered mandāra blossoms on him,
And gladly offered whole-hearted worship.
The 'pure-living' gods rejoiced and were glad
That a Tathāgata had arisen.
Though they had got rid of lustful delight,
They still were pleased because of the Doctrine,
For the Buddha brought liberation to
Living beings sunk in suffering's ocean.
Sumeru, the precious king of mountains,
Which solidly supports this mighty earth,
Was tossed about by the wind of virtue
When Bodhisattva appeared in the world.
Every place was shaken by a great quake,
Like a boat that is drummed by wind and wave.
A faint, light perfume of sandalwood
Streamed through space on the current of the wind,
And a wealth of many lotus blossoms
Tumbled down commingled in profusion.
From the sky came down heavenly garments
Which gave wonderful pleasure to the touch.
The sun and moon redoubled and increased
Their brightness many times beyond normal.
The rays of all the fires throughout the world
Without fuel blazed up brightly of themselves.
Pure water, in the clear, refreshing wells,

Sprang up spontaneously here and there.
The crowds of maids in the inner palace
Were amazed and exclaimed at the wonder.
They ran there together to drink and bathe.
In all arose calm and delightful thoughts.
A countless number of nature spirits,
Delighting in the Law, gathered like clouds.
In the garden of Lumbinī
Everywhere amid the forest
Many strange and wonderful flowers
Bloomed profusely out of season.
Wicked and fierce sorts of living beings
All together conceived kindness of heart.
All diseases and sickness in the world
Went away of themselves, without treatment.
The tumultuous cries of birds and beasts
Were muted and silent; there was no sound.
In the ten thousand streams, the current stopped;
Muddy water became limpid and clear.
In the sky there was no shade of a cloud.
The gods' drum sounded of its own accord.
Everyone in the entire universe
Obtained ease, serenity and pleasure.
It was like a ravaged, harassed country
Which suddenly obtains a wise ruler.
The reason that Bodhisattva was born
Was to save the world's masses from distress.

Chapter Fourteen: The Decision to Preach the Doctrine

He had fully achieved no 'I' or 'mine',
As when fuel is used up a fire dies out.
He had performed what was to be performed.
He had attained true enlightenment.

He had fully probed the ultimate truth,
And entered the house of the great seers.
Darkness receded and brightness was born.
Motion stopped, and all was still and silent.
He had reached the inexhaustible Truth.
All-knowledge shone out clearly and brightly.
The great seer's virtues were pure and rich.
For him the earth shook and quaked everywhere.
All the universe was clear and brilliant.
Gods, dragons and spirits gathered in clouds,
Playing divine music in open space,
Thereby offering worship to the Doctrine.
A gentle breeze arose, fresh and cooling.
A fragrant rain fell from a cloudless sky.
Exquisite flowers bloomed out of season.
Sweet fruits ripened contrary to their times.
Gigantic blossoms of Mandāravas
And all kinds of precious heavenly flowers
Descended in confusion from the sky,
In worship of the solitary saint.
All the different sorts of living beings
Turned towards each other with kindly hearts.
Their fears were entirely melted away,
And no one had thoughts of anger or pride.
Living beings throughout all worldly realms
Were all the same as the undefiled man.
All the gods rejoiced in liberation
And the evil paths were at peace a while.
The passions were suspended for a time.
The moon of wisdom grew ever brighter.
When the seers of the Ikṣvāku clan,
Who had been born among the gods,
Beheld the Buddha arise in the world

Their bodies were suffused with rejoicing.
When, from their celestial palaces
They had rained down the blossoms in worship,
All the gods, spirits, demons and dragons
With the same voice praised the Buddha's virtues.
Worldly men, when they beheld the worship
And heard the voices reciting praises,
Were each and all in their turn overjoyed,
Could not control themselves, and danced and skipped.
It was only Māra, king among gods,
Whose heart was troubled by a great anguish.
The Buddha continued for seven days
Meditating, in purity of mind,
Examining the Enlightenment Tree,
Gazing at it with calm, unwinking eyes.
→ "Resting for support on this place I have
Fulfilled the vows I made in former lives,
And reside in the doctrine of no-self."
Regarding beings with the Buddha-eye,
He felt great compassion swell in his heart.
He wished to make them attain purity.
In wrong views of greed, hate and ignorance
They drifted about, and their hearts were drowned.
Liberation was most profound and fine,
But then through what means could he proclaim it?
He rejected methods of exertion,
Intending to remain still in silence.
Then he recalled his original vows,
And again desired to preach the Doctrine.
He looked at living beings and wondered
"Who will alleviate their afflictions?"
The God Brahma, understanding his thoughts,
Feeling he should ask him to preach the Law,

Everywhere released his Brahma-splendour,
In order to save suffering beings.
He came and saw the solitary saint's
Traits of the doctrine-preaching Great Person,
His wonderful intent all apparent,
Dwelling in knowledge of reality,
Free from the troubles of impediments,
Without any vain or deceitful thoughts.
Respectfully, rejoicing in his heart,
He joined his palms and implored him, saying
" What fortune, what happiness for people,
To encounter the great World-Honoured One!
Among all the kinds of living beings
With minds fouled by dust and confused by muck,
There are some who suffer from grave passions
And some whose passions are light and feeble.
The World-Honoured One has already crossed
Birth-and-death's vast ocean of suffering.
Please now rescue and ferry across those
Many living beings who sink and drown.
Even as a righteous worldly person,
When he makes a profit, shares his goods around,
The World-Honoured has the profit of Truth
And ought to deliver living beings.
Many common men seek their own profit;
Few seek to profit both others and self.
I pray you to shed kindness and pity
And do the hardest of the world's hard things."
Thus having exhorted and implored him,
He took leave back to the Brahma-heaven.
The Buddha, thinking of Brahma's request,
Was pleased and admired his sincerity.
His heart of great compassion was nourished

And his desire to preach the Law increased.
He thought that he should go and beg for food.
The four kings each offered a bowl to him.
Tathāgata, for the sake of the Law,
Received the four and joined them into one.
At that time some merchants were passing by.
A good friend, a heavenly spirit, said
" The great seer, the solitary saint,
Is residing in that mountain forest.
He is the world's noblest field of merit.
You should go and offer worship to him."
They obeyed the command with great gladness
And offered the first meal in donation.
Having eaten, he deliberated,
" Who is worthy to hear the Doctrine first?
Nobody but Arāḍa Kālāma [2]
And also Udraka Rāmaputra [2]
Is worthy to receive the True Doctrine.
However, now they are already dead.
Next in order are the five mendicants [3]
Who should hear the first preaching of the Law."
Wishing to preach the law of cessation,
Like the sun's rays dispelling the darkness,
He set out on the way to Benares,
The place in which the ancient seers lived.
Gazing evenly with the ox-king's eyes,
With a lion's quiet and steady pace,
For the sake of saving living beings
He went on towards the Kāśi city.
Step by step, watching like the king of beasts,
He glanced around the Enlightenment Grove.

Chapter Eighteen : Anāthapiṇḍaka presents the Jetavana Grove

(Anāthapiṇḍaka, a rich merchant, is just about to purchase a teaching grove and present it to the Buddha.)

The Buddha understood the elder's heart.
Now he had awakened great charity.
He was without taint and free from clinging,
And kept living beings well in his mind.
" You have already perceived the real truth.
Your simple heart loves deeds of charity.
Money and wealth are transient treasure.
You had better make gifts of them quickly.
When a treasure chamber has been burned down,
Though things taken out in time are precious,
The wise man, aware of their transiency,
Gives out his wealth, widely doing kindness.
The greedy miser hoards them grudgingly,
Fearing he will have nothing left to use,
But still not afraid of impermanence.
He loses in vain and adds to his grief.
Give at the right time to the right vessel.
Like a soldier nearing the enemy
Who, giving, is able to do battle,
So is the man who is brave in wisdom.
The generous man is loved by the people.
His good reputation spreads far and wide.
The virtuous delight in his friendship.
Throughout his life his heart is always glad.
He is without remorse and without fear.
He is not born among the hungry ghosts.
This, then, is the maturing of the flower.
The fruit is difficult to imagine.
While you revolve in the six destinies

No companion surpasses charity.
If you are born as a god or a man,
You will receive service from the people.
If you are born on the animal path,
Charity will ripen to happiness.
Wisdom develops still concentration
That is unsupported and unconditioned.
Even though you reach the immortal way,
You still complete it through generous giving,
For kind giving is its precondition.
Training yourself in the eight attainments,
Your heart rejoices in contemplation,
You are firmly fixed in contemplation.
Absorption is the increase of insight
Which regards birth and decay rightly.
Having looked rightly at birth and decay
You will afterwards get liberation.
Those who in charity renounce their wealth
Cleanse away avarice and attachment.
Giving in compassion and respect,
They drive away envy, hatred and pride.
When you clearly perceive charity's fruit,
The ignorance of non-giving is removed
And all bonds and passions are extinguished.
This proceeds from kindness and charity.
You ought to understand that charity
Is therefore the cause of liberation.
It is like a sapling which a man plants
For the sake of its shade, flowers and fruit.
In the same way generous charity
Has the happy fruit of Great Nirvāṇa.
In giving away unenduring wealth
You obtain enduring fruit in reward.

If you give food, you get strength in return.
Give clothes and you get a beautiful form.
If you establish religious houses
You will be fully endowed with all fruits.
Some bestow to gratify the five lusts,
Some to gratify their greed for great wealth.
Some give for the sake of reputation.
Some seek the delights of birth in heaven.
Some would escape from poverty and pain.
Only you give without private motive.
The paramount degree of charity
Is disinterested and non-grasping.
Your heart has magnanimous intentions.
You had better accomplish them quickly.
Though stupid, clinging thoughts come wandering
The eye of purity opens again."
The elder received the Buddha's teaching,
And his kindly thoughts became still brighter.

2. EARNEST FAITH

Dharmapada, Chapter Four

1. Faith, conscience, good conduct and thought are wealth.
   These qualities excellent men commend.
   This way is preached by the knowing and wise.
   Such as these ascend to the heavenly realms.
2. The stupid neglect the way to heaven.
   Neither do they praise generosity.
   Those who have faith, who give, who help the good
   Go on from here and arrive at that peace.
3. The faithful are the leaders of true men.
   Thinking of the Law, they reside in peace.
   People near them are uplifted in thought.
   The life of wisdom is the best of lives.
4. By faith the Way can be attained.
   The doctrine leads to cessation.
   From hearing, wisdom is obtained.
   In what is reached there is clearness.
5. Faith can cross over the abyss.
   Acceptance is the boat's captain.
   Diligence gets rid of suffering.
   Insight reaches the other shore.
6. The man with faith and good conduct
   Is commended by the holy.
   Those who like the uncreated
   Are released from all that binds them.
7. By faith, by keeping the precepts,
   And thoughts of insight proceeding,
   The strong man passes beyond hate

And so is freed from the abyss.
8. The faithful fulfil the precepts
As well as long life and insight.
In whatever place they may walk,
They are sustained by everyone.
9. Compared with the world's benefits,
Insight and faith are the wisest.
This wealth is the highest treasure.
Worldly goods are impermanent.
10. He who likes to see the true ones
Listens gladly to the Doctrine
And sheds the filth of avarice.
This is what it means to have faith.
11. Faith can cross over the river.
Its blessings are hard to plunder.
They ward off and stop the robber.
Wilderness hermits are happy.
12. The faithless do not train themselves.
They like to peel and strip right words,
Like one who digs to get water
And, scooping the spring, stirs up mud.
13. The worthy man trains in wisdom
And likes to look on the pure stream,
Like one good at getting water
Who takes care not to disturb it.
14. The faithful do not taint others.
Let the worthy know the gentle.
You should learn from those who are good
And keep far away from the bad.
15. Faith is a vehicle for us.
No one knows how much it carries.
Taming self is even higher
Than taming a great elephant.

16. Faith is wealth, the precepts are wealth;
    Conscience and shame are also wealth.
    Hearing is wealth, giving is wealth,
    And insight is the seventh wealth.
17. Follow faith and keep the precepts;
    Be always pure; regard the Law;
    Be wise, and so walk with profit;
    Receive humbly; do not forget.
18. Throughout life you will have this wealth,
    Whether you are man or woman.
    With it you will never be poor.
    The worthy understand this truth.

3. EQUALITY
Mahālaṅkāra Śāstra, Chapter Six

This work is a chain of edifying stories with prose narrative but verse dialogue and moralizing. It embodies material from diverse sources, and is probably the work of more than one author. The Chinese translation has been wrongly attributed to Kumārajīva. The theme of the following passage—the absurdity of the caste system—was a favourite one with Buddhist preachers.

A low-caste man named Nidhi was carrying a jar of manure on his back when he heard that the Buddha was in the town. He detoured through the back streets and alleys to avoid bringing his impurity before the Blessed One. But the Buddha knew his thoughts and pursued him, appearing again and again in the street before him. Finally, when Nidhi had no way of getting past, the Buddha asked him if he wanted to enter the religious life, and recited these stanzas:

1. The Tathāgata does not examine
   Race, caste, social position or riches.
   In all beings he only looks at deeds
   And seeds of goodness planted in the past.
2. Those who are bound fast by all the passions
   Do not attain complete liberation.
   Being born, growing old, disease and death,
   Suffering and pleasure are common to all.
3. I ask you why should the Brahmans alone
   Be able to attain liberation?
   Cannot the rest of mankind reach it too?
   Literature and writing, words and sounds,—
   The other castes can understand them too.
4. It is like a ford for crossing a stream,
   Which is not just for the use of Brahmans

But at the service of the other castes.
Is the performance of all acts and works
Possible to the Brahman caste alone
And impossible to the rest of man?

5. Now the proper course for you is simply
To believe me and leave the household life.
In this Buddha-doctrine of mine there is
Compassion without discrimination.
It is not the same as the infidels
Who possess occult and concealed doctrines.

6. I save all, equally, impartially.
The Buddha's doctrine has no short measure.
I preach the Law without partiality.
I show the Right Way to all, equally,
For the sake of every living being.
I construct the peaceful, secure Right Road.

7. It may be compared to a great market,
A market where the goods are sold to all.
The market of my doctrine is the same.
I do not choose between castes and surnames,
But accept rich and noble, poor and low.

8. It resembles a stream of pure water.
The nobility and the priestly caste,
The farmers, the merchants, the serfs and slaves,—
None are prevented or prohibited;
Neither men nor animals are debarred;
All and everyone can come there to drink.

9. It is the same way with my doctrine, too,
For I do not make distinctions,
You men and women of the homeless life.
Universally for those in the world,
For men and gods, I am the great healer.

4. RATNAKŪṬA'S HYMN TO THE BUDDHA

This poem and the following one are from Kumārajīva's translation of the *Vimalakīrti Nirdeśa Sūtra*, one of the most popular expositions of the bodhisattva's life. The hero is the elder Vimalakīrti of Vaiśāli, a householder bodhisattva whose insight is superior to that of all the monks. In the first chapter, an elder's son Ratnakūṭa, with five hundred companions, comes to see the Buddha, who miraculously manifests all the worlds for his guests' benefit. Ratnakūṭa then recites this hymn in praise of the Buddha.

1. To him whose eyes are pure, long and broad as a blue lotus,
   Whose mind is pure, having passed through all the exaltations,
   Who for long has amassed pure deeds, whose fame is unbounded,
   Who conducts the people to peace, to him I bow my head.
2. Already we have seen the Great Saint through his magic changes
   Show forth the infinite lands of the entire ten quarters,
   With all the Buddhas in them discoursing on the Doctrine,
   All of which has been both seen and heard by everyone here.
3. The King of Truth's doctrine-power surpasses common beings'.
   He continually bestows the wealth of truth on all;
   He distinguishes well the marks of all the elements;
   He rests immovable in the highest reality.
4. He has achieved the mastery of all the elements.
   Therefore I bow my head before this king of the doctrine.
   He preaches that the elements neither are nor are not,
   That all the elements arise through cause and condition.

5. There is no self, there is no deed, there is no receiver.
   Neither do actions of good and evil become extinct.
   Since under the Buddha Tree he first forced Māra to yield,
   Obtained the nectar of peace, and achieved enlightenment,
   He has had no thought, perception, feeling or mentation
   And yet on all sides he breaks and subdues the outsiders.
6. Three times he has turned the Doctrine's Wheel in the universe.
   From the beginning this wheel has always been wholly pure.
   That gods and men gained enlightenment was proof of this fact.[4]
   In this way the Three Treasures were made visible in the world.[5]
7. With this wonderful doctrine he rescues common beings.
   They receive it once, do not lapse, and are ever at peace.
   The great prince of physicians saves from age, disease and death.
   Men should revere the boundless virtue of his sea of Truth.
8. He is as unmoved by blame or praise as Mount Sumeru.
   He treats the good and the evil with equal compassion.
   The workings of his heart are as impartial as the sky.
   Who that hears does not honour and accept the gem of men?
9. Now we offer the Blessed One this humble parasol
   And in it he shows forth the three thousand realms of our world.
   The palaces in which the gods and dragon spirits live,
   The palaces of the fairies, the homes of the demons,—
10. We saw everything that exists anywhere in the world.
    In kindness he of the ten powers showed these transformations.
    The assembly, seeing this wonder, all praise the Buddha.
    Now I bow my head to the Honoured One of the three worlds.

11. The Great Saint, the Doctrine-King, is the assembly's refuge.
    We cleanse our hearts in seeing the Buddha and all rejoice.
    Everyone sees the World-Honoured One present before him.
    Such are his magic powers and his uncommon qualities.[6]
12. The Buddha proclaims and preaches the Doctrine with one voice;
    Each living being understands according to his kind.
    Each says that the World-Honoured One speaks in his own language.
    Such are his magic powers and his uncommon qualities.
13. The Buddha proclaims and preaches the Doctrine with one voice,
    And yet adapts it to what each being can understand.
    Everywhere men accept it and acquire its benefits.
    Such are his magic powers and his uncommon qualities.
14. The Buddha proclaims and preaches the Doctrine with one voice;
    Some have fear and consternation, some delight and are glad,
    Some loathe impurity, and some eradicate their doubts.
    Such are his magic powers and his uncommon qualities.
15. I bow my head to him with the ten powers and great valour.
    I bow my head before him who has attained fearlessness.
    I bow my head to him who holds the special attributes.
    I bow my head before the great path-finder and leader.
16. I bow my head to the cutter of all bonds and fetters.
    I bow my head to him who has attained the Other Shore.
    I bow my head to the liberator of all the worlds.
    I bow to one who is ever beyond birth-and-death's road.

17. He knows all omens of living beings' pasts and futures.
    He is well emancipated from all the elements.
    He is as detached from the world as a lotus blossom.
    Always he has well entered the course of void and stillness.
    Without hindrance he penetrates all the elements' traits.
    I bow my head to him who like space depends on nothing.

5. THE BODHISATTVA'S HOUSEHOLD

Vimalakīrti Nirdeśa Sūtra, Chapter Eight
Chinese translation by Kumārajīva, A.D. 406

Before Mañjuśrī and the great assembly arrived to converse with him, Vimalakīrti had sent all his household away and cleared all the furniture out of the house. When he was asked about his household, he replied in this gāthā.

1. Wisdom is the bodhisattva's mother.
   Appropriate method is his father.
   The guides and leaders of the multitudes
   Are each and all brought forth from these parents.
2. Enjoyment of the doctrine is his wife.
   Sympathy and mercy are his daughters.
   Goodwill and sincerity are his sons.
   Ultimate void and stillness are his house.
3. His crowd of disciples is the passions,
   Which obey the directions of his will.
   His friends are the Wings of Enlightenment
   Through whom he grows to true enlightenment.
4. The perfections are his religious friends.
   The four inducements are his singing girls
   Who sing and chant the words of the doctrine,
   And this melody serves as his music.
5. The formulas are his parks and gardens.
   The untainted elements are his trees.
   The wish for bodhi forms their pure, fine flowers.
   Liberation and insight are their fruit.
6. The bathing pool of eight liberations
   Is filled deep with meditation's water

And strewn with the seven flowers of pureness.
The bather is the undefiled person.

7. The five powers are elephants and horses.
   The Great Vehicle is his chariot,
   Which is driven by singleness of mind
   And travels along the eightfold right road.

8. The marks provide his figure's ornaments.
   All the minor signs adorn his body.
   Contrition is the garment that he wears.
   A deep mind is his headdress of flowers.

9. His riches are the seven precious things.
   To teach the Law is the interest from them.
   To behave according to the teaching
   And transfer the merit is his great gain.

10. The four absorptions are his bed and seat
    Which are produced from a life of pureness.
    Ample learning and increase of wisdom
    Are the music by which he is wakened.

11. His food is the nectar of the doctrine.
    The taste of liberation is his sauce.
    He washes in the bath of a pure mind.
    The sections of the rule are his lotion.

12. He exterminates the bandit passions.
    None can surpass him in courage or strength.
    He subdues the four classes of devils
    And hoists victory's flag in the field-of-Truth.

13. He knows that there is no birth or decay
    Yet is born in order to show others.
    He manifests himself in all countries
    And like the sun he is seen everywhere.

14. In the ten quarters he honours and serves
    Unnumbered millions of Tathāgatas.
    In his thoughts he conceives no distinction

Between the Buddhas and his own person.
15. Though he knows that all the Buddha-countries
And ordinary beings are empty,
Yet he always cultivates a Pure Land
For the instruction of common beings.
16. The bodhisattva with power of no-fear,
Can fully manifest in one moment
All the kinds of living beings that are,
With their forms and voice and behaviour.
17. He is aware of the Māras' affairs
And appears to follow their practices.
By his wisdom of efficient good means
He can manifest them all at his will.
18. Sometimes he appears old, sick or dying
In order to mature common beings.
He knows well that all is like a phantom.
His understanding meets no obstacles.
19. Sometimes he shows the fire that ends an age,
Which utterly consumes heaven and earth.
Its blaze demonstrates transitoriness
To beings with notions of permanence.
20. When countless millions of living beings
All come and invite the bodhisattva
He goes to all their homes at the same time
And converts them to seek the Buddha's Way.
21. Texts of prescriptions and books of formulas,
Skills, and all kinds of mechanical arts,—
All of these he produces and uses
To benefit ordinary beings.
22. In order to resolve people's errors,
He enters the monastic life in all
The many religious sects of the world
Yet does not fall into perverted views.

23. Sometimes he acts as god of sun and moon,
    Or as King Brahma, ruler of the world.
    Sometimes he acts as the earth or water.
    Sometimes, again, he acts as wind or fire.
24. Whenever there is a plague in an age
    He manifests himself as drugs and herbs
    And whoever swallows these medicines
    Is cured of disease and purged of poisons.
25. When there is a famine in any age
    He manifests himself as food and drink.
    First he delivers people from hunger
    And then he tells them about the doctrine.
26. If there are arms and armies in an age
    He rouses goodwill and pity towards them,
    And he converts all those living beings
    To live in a state free from contention.
27. When there is a great array of battle
    And the armies are raised in equal strength
    The bodhisattva shows his dreadful force,
    Subdues them, and brings concord and peace.
28. Throughout each and every land and country
    To every place where beings are in hell
    He goes in haste, and having arrived there
    He labours to relieve their afflictions.
29. Throughout each and every land and country
    Where animal beings eat each other
    There he manifests himself in life
    In order to give benefit to them.
30. He appears to indulge in the five lusts
    But he also appears to meditate,
    And thus he confuses the devils' minds
    So that they miss their opportunities.
31. A lotus blossom that grows in a fire

    Has to be described as a rarity.
    One who lives amid lust yet meditates
    Constitutes a still greater miracle.
32. Sometimes he appears to be a harlot
    To attract all those who are fond of sex.
    First he draws them in with the hook of lust,
    Then leads them into the Buddha's wisdom.
33. Sometimes he is a city magistrate.
    Sometimes he is a leader of merchants,
    A state teacher, or a great minister,
    In order to profit living beings.
34. For all who are in poverty and need
    He appears as an endless store of wealth,
    And takes the chance to exhort and guide them
    So that they aspire to enlightenment.
35. To the self-minded, arrogant and proud
    He shows himself as a man of great strength
    To reduce and subdue their arrogance
    And establish them in the supreme Way.
36. With the multitudes who are timorous
    He stays before them and reassures them.
    First he confers fearlessness upon them.
    Then he brings them to aspire to the Way.
37. Sometimes he appears free from lewd desires
    As a hermit with five magic powers
    To teach and guide ordinary beings
    And set them in precepts, patience and love.
38. If he sees anyone who needs servants
    He appears and acts as a serving man.
    After he has satisfied the man's needs
    He then awakens his mind to the Way.
39. In accordance with what people require
    He gets them to enter the Buddha's Way.

     By his power of efficient good means
     He can provide them with all that they need.
40. Thus his enlightenment is infinite.
     His practices are innumerable.
     His wisdom and insight are limitless.
     He liberates a countless multitude.
41. Even supposing that all the Buddhas
     Were to sing the praises of his virtue
     Through millions of ages without number,
     They still wouldn't be able to finish.
42. Who that has heard such a doctrine as this
     Would not have the wish for enlightenment,
     Except for some people of no account
     Who are without wisdom, stupid and dim?

6. THE KĀŚYAPA-PARIVARTA SŪTRA

This scripture, one of the *Ratnakūṭa* collection, consists of about one hundred parables in answer to Kāśyapa's questions to the Buddha. The following verses are taken from the Chinese version by Dānapāla, which was translated about A.D. 980.

> It is like two trees rubbing together.
> When the wind blows it generates a fire,
> And no sooner is the fire ignited
> Than in its turn it burns up the two trees.
> Even so is the true contemplation.
> It produces the power of insight
> Which, the instant it has arisen,
> Turns and consumes the true contemplation.
>
> It is like a wheel-turning monarch's maid
> Who is favoured by the love of the king
> And afterwards gives birth to a male child.
> He too belongs to the nobility.
> It is the same with the bodhisattva
> When first he aspires to enlightenment.
> Though his virtuous deeds are poor and few,
> He uses good means to instruct beings.
> Although he has not passed beyond the three worlds,
> His performance is called the Buddha-mind.
> He is called a true son of the Buddha.
>
> It is just like the kalaviṅka bird.[7]
> Even while it is still inside the egg,
> Though it has never seen body or form,

Yet, being different from other birds,
It emits fine, exquisite melodies
So that men always take pleasure in it.
Even so is the son of the Buddha
When he first aspires to enlightenment
And has not emerged from the passions' womb.
Not any one of the private buddhas,
No one of the multitudes of hearers,
Can be ranked in comparison with him.
He is turned towards serene happiness.
He uses good means for beings' welfare.
He is pure, kind and merciful in thought,
And radiates fine, exquisite music.

It is like the Himālaya Mountains
Which produce wonderful medicines
That remedy every sort of disease.
Whenever anyone swallows these drugs
He is cured and never troubled again.
It is even so with the Buddha's son.
He grows the herb of wonderful wisdom
Which is the remedy for all mankind
Infirm with the passions, birth and old age.
He applies it impartially to all.
Whenever anyone partakes of it,
He has no more doubts and becomes certain.

As a man who is seriously ill,
Long afflicted and without remedy,
In the end succumbs to impermanence,
Though he takes an excellent medicine,
Even so are ordinary beings
Who are always infected with passions.

Though they delight in great erudition
They will not escape downfall for ever.

It may be likened to a worldly man.
When he washes and bathes his body clean,
Anointing it with good and fragrant oils,
Adorning his head with a flowered headdress
And clothing his body in white garments,
He is called the son of a noble clan.
It is even so with the homeless monk.
For ever pure in conduct and virtue,
Being clothed in the garments of the Law,
Perfect in deportment and appearance,
He is called the true son of the Buddha.

7. *THE TEACHER OF RELIGION*

Saddharma-Puṇḍarīka Sūtra, Chapter Ten
Chinese translation by Kumārajīva, c. A.D. 400

1. When any man goes to preach this scripture,
   Let him enter the Tathāgata's house
   And put on the Tathāgata's garment
   And sit down in the Tathāgata's seat.
   Let him be fearless in the assembly
   And preach widely and intelligently.
2. Great sympathy and pity are the house.
   Gentleness and patience are the garment.
   The seat is voidness of all elements.
   Let him take this place to preach the doctrine.
3. If when a man is preaching this scripture
   There are men who abuse him with foul words
   And attack him with knives, sticks, tiles and stones,
   He should bear it for thought of the Buddha.
4. In a hundred thousand million countries
   I manifest my pure, stable body.
   During numberless millions of ages
   I preach the Doctrine to living beings.
5. If after I have entered extinction
   Any person will proclaim this scripture
   I will send four kinds of phantom beings,—
   Men and women of the homeless life,
   Besides lay men and women of pure faith,—
   To worship the teacher of the Doctrine,
   To lead and guide ordinary beings,
   And gather them to listen to the Law.

6. If someone wants to do him injury
   With knives and sticks and also tiles and stones,
   Then I will send out my phantom beings
   To be his defenders and protection.
7. If a man who is a preacher of the Law
   Is living alone in the wilderness,
   In solitude without a human sound,
   Reading and chanting this scriptural text,
8. At that time I will manifest to him
   My immaculate, resplendent body.
   If he forgets a chapter or phrase
   I will clarify his understanding.
9. Such people as cultivate this virtue,
   Whether preaching to the four assemblies
   Or reciting scriptures in solitude,
   Will all get the vision of my body.
10. When a person lives in the wilderness
    I will send gods and dragon kings to him,
    Demons, and ghosts and spirits, and so on,
    For an assembly to hear the Doctrine.
11. This man delights in preaching the Doctrine.
    His intellect has no impediments.
    Because he keeps all the Buddhas in mind
    He is able to please great multitudes.
12. Those intimate with the doctrine-teacher
    Swiftly attain the bodhisattva's way.
    They train under this teacher's direction
    And see Buddhas numerous as Ganges' sands.

8. THE ETERNAL BUDDHA

Saddharma-Puṇḍarīka Sūtra

Chapter Sixteen (Chinese Text), which corresponds to
Chapter Fifteen (Sanskrit Text)

1. Since the time when I became a Buddha,
   The number of ages which have gone by
   Is innumerable hundreds of millions,
   Numberless hundreds of billions of years.
2. Since innumerable ages ago
   I have always preached the Law to instruct
   Numberless billions of living beings
   That they might come into the Buddha's Way.
3. For the salvation of living beings
   I show Nirvāṇa through skilful means
   Yet I do not really become extinct
   But dwell here for ever, preaching the Law.
4. I remain in this place eternally,
   But due to my supernatural powers
   Living beings perverted by error
   Do not see me, although they are near me.
5. The multitudes look on me as extinct,
   Universally worship my relics,
   All cherish devoted admiration,
   And conceive a longing to behold me.
6. When beings have believed and submitted,
   And are upright, mild and gentle of mind,
   Sincerely wishing to see a Buddha,
   Not begrudging their own bodies or lives,
   Then I and the company of my monks

Come out together on the Vulture Peak.[8]

7. At that time I inform living beings
That I live here for ever, not extinct.
Because of my power of efficient means
It seems that I perish, but I do not.

8. Where living beings in other countries
Are respectful and disposed to faith,
I am present there in their midst
In order to preach the supreme Doctrine.
You people, not having heard of this fact,
Simply consider that I am extinct.

9. I regard all ordinary beings
Living sunk in the sea of suffering,
But I do not manifest my body.
Thus I rouse their thirst and expectation.
Because of their hearts' longing devotion
I then come out and preach the Law for them.

10. Such, then, are my supernatural powers.
During an endless number of ages
I am ever on the Vulture Peak
And in all my other dwelling-places.

11. Though living beings see the age's end,
When the great conflagration is raging,
This land of mine is tranquil and secure,
Always populated with gods and men.

12. Living beings roam and amuse themselves
In gardens and groves, halls and pavilions,
Which are adorned with gems of many kinds
And gem-trees with many blossoms and fruit.

13. The gods striking on their heavenly drums
Constantly make all kinds of fine music
And shower down mandārava blossoms
Over the Buddha and great assembly.

14. My Pure Land does not suffer destruction,
    Yet the masses see it consumed by flames
    And as if it were entirely replete
    With sorrow, terror, pain and affliction.
15. All these sinful ordinary beings
    By cause and circumstance of evil deeds
    Pass through an endless number of ages
    Without hearing the Three Jewels mentioned.
16. All those who have cultivated virtue,
    Who are gentle and of upright disposition,
    Will each see the vision of my body
    Present here and proclaiming the Doctrine.
17. Sometimes for the sake of this assembly
    I preach that the Buddha's life is endless.
    To those who have seen the Buddha for long
    I preach that a Buddha is hard to find.
18. Such as this is the power of my wisdom.
    My insight's light which shines without limit,
    And my lifetime of numberless ages,
    Were gained through long cultivation of deeds.
19. Let everyone among you who is wise,
    Conceive no doubt in regard to this fact.
    Let your doubts cease and be dead for ever.
    The Buddha's word is really true, not false.
20. As a doctor who is skilled in good means
    Though really alive, has his death announced
    In order to cure his demented son,
    And cannot be accused of deception,
21. I, too, being the father of the world,
    Who relieves all suffering and trouble,
    Though really alive, announce my decease
    For the sake of perverted common men,
22. Because if people see me constantly

>   They may conceive arrogant, careless thoughts,
>   Abandon themselves, cling to the five lusts
>   And fall into the evil destinies.
> 23. I always know whether living beings
>   Walk in the Way or don't walk in the Way,
>   And according to how they may be saved
>   I preach different kinds of doctrine to them.
> 24. In each case I ask myself this question:
>   ' By what can I get these living beings
>   To go into supreme enlightenment
>   And quickly mature their Buddha bodies?'

9. UNIVERSAL MERCY

Saddharma-Puṇḍarīka, Chapter Twenty-five (Chinese Text)
(This corresponds to Chapter Twenty-four in the Sanskrit Text)

1. "World-Honoured One, endowed with wondrous signs,
   Now I wish to ask my question again;
   How did that Buddha's son come to be called
   'Regarder of the Voices of the World'?"
2. The Honoured One, possessed of wondrous signs,
   Answered Akṣayamati in these lines:
   "You should listen to the deeds of Kwannon;
   How well he responds to every quarter,
3. His immense vow, profound as the ocean,
   The unthinkable ages he has passed
   In serving many millions of Buddhas,
   And the great, pure vows he has put forth,
4. These I will briefly indicate to you.
   If you hear his name and see his body,
   And then diligently keep him in mind,
   It will extinguish all your suffering.
5. If someone with the intent to murder
   Throws you down into a great pit of fire,
   Let your thought dwell on the power of Kwannon
   And the pit of fire will become a pond.
6. If you are cast adrift on the vast sea,
   Afflicted by sea monsters and demons,
   Let your thought dwell on the power of Kwannon
   And waves and billows cannot submerge you.
7. If you are on the peak of Sumeru
   And someone pushes you and throws you down,

Let your thought dwell on the power of Kwannon
And you will stay in mid-space like the sun.

8. If you are pursued by evil persons
And fall down on to the Diamond Mountains,
Let your thought dwell on the power of Kwannon
And not a single hair can suffer harm.

9. If you are surrounded by enemies
Each sword in hand and intent on murder,
Let your thought dwell on the power of Kwannon
And instantly all will turn kind-hearted.

10. If you are suffering a king's harshness,
Nearing execution and your life's end,
Let your thought dwell on the power of Kwannon
And at once the sword will break in pieces.

11. If the jailkeeper locks you in a yoke,
Manacles your hands, and shackles your feet,
Let your thought dwell on the power of Kwannon.
The chains will drop off and let you go free.

12. If there are spells, curses, poisons or drugs
Which are intended to work harm on you,
Let your thought dwell on the power of Kwannon.
They will revert and stick to their authors.

13. If you should encounter malignant ghouls,
Venomous dragons, or evil spirits,
Let your thought dwell on the power of Kwannon
And not one of them will dare to hurt you.

14. If you should be surrounded by wild beast,
Sharp of tooth and claw, and terrifying,
Let your thought dwell on the power of Kwannon
And they will flee in every direction.

15. If lizards, vipers, cobras, scorpions,
Breathe out poison, smoke and flame upon you,
Let your thought dwell on the power of Kwannon

And they will turn and flee with sudden shrieks.
16. If thunderclaps and lightning split the clouds,
    If hail falls and a great torrent pours down,
    Let your thought dwell on the power of Kwannon
    And in no time they will have dispersed.
17. If a living being suffers distress
    And unending pain torments his body,
    Kwannon's wonderful power of wisdom
    Can relieve him of the world's afflictions.
18. He is endowed with miraculous powers
    And widely skilled in knowledge and good means.
    In all the countries of the ten quarters
    There is no place he does not show himself.
19. The various kinds of evil destiny
    (Hell, ghosts, and animal existence),
    The pain of birth, old age, disease and death,—
    Bit by bit he will extinguish them all.
20. He sees in truth, he in purity,
    He sees with enormous intelligence,
    He sees with mercy, he sees with kindness!
    Ever pray to him, ever adore him!
21. Undefiled and pure illumination,
    Sun of insight which shatters all darkness,
    Subduer of wind and fire's disasters,
    Universal light which shines on the world!
22. Goodness based on mercy is the thunder;
    Compassion is the excellent great cloud
    Which pours down the Doctrine's rain of nectar,
    Extinguishing the flames of the passions.
23. If you are passing through a case at court,
    Or are trembling in the line of battle,
    Let your thought dwell on the power of Kwannon
    And all enemies will flee and scatter.

24. Kwanzeon has a most exquisite voice,
    Voice of Brahma, voice of the ocean tides,
    Voice which excels all voices of the world.
    Therefore let our thoughts always dwell on him.
25. Remember, remember, permit no doubt.
    World-Voice-Regarder is pure and holy.
    For all in pain and torment, death and woe,
    He is indeed a refuge and support.
26. He is endowed with all fine qualities.
    His kindly eye watches over beings.
    He stores blessings boundless as the ocean.
    Therefore let us bow in adoration."

10. IN PRAISE OF THE BUDDHA

Larger Sukhāvatī-Vyūha Sūtra

Saṅghavarman's translation

When Amitābha was still the Bodhisattva Dharmākara, he studied under the Buddha Lokeśvararāja. This is the hymn which he recited in praise of that Buddha.

1. Shining face most awe-inspiring!
   Pervading power unlimited!
   Such radiant brilliance as this
   Is quite beyond comparison.
   The sun, the moon and precious stones,
   Though blazing with dazzling splendour,
   Are cast into obscurity
   Just as if they were cakes of black ink.
2. The Tathāgata's form and face
   Are without equal in the world.
   The All-Enlightened One's great voice
   Resounds throughout the universe.
   His morality, his energy,
   His absorption and his insight,—
   These sublime virtues have no peer;
   They are most excellent and rare.
3. Deeply, clearly, he meditates
   On the Buddha's ocean of truth.
   He exhausts its depths and secrets
   And explores its shores and reaches.
   The Honoured One is ever free
   From ignorance and lust and hate.

    He is the lion of brave men.
    His wondrous virtue is endless.
4. His merit is ample and great;
    His insight is deep and subtle.
    His overaweing radiance
    Shakes the thousand universes.
    I resolve to be a Buddha
    Like the holy King of the Truth.
    I will cross over birth-and-death
    And will liberate all beings.
5. In charity, in mind-control,
    Restraint, forbearance, energy,
    As well as in contemplation
    And in insight I shall excel.
    I vow to become a Buddha
    And everywhere carry out these vows.
    All those who are in fear and dread
    I will establish in great peace.
6. Though the Buddhas in existence
    Were a hundred thousand million,
    Innumerable great holy men,
    As numerous as the Ganges' sands,
    To serve and worship each and all
    These innumerable Buddhas
    Is less than seeking Buddhahood,
    Firmly, rightly, not regressing.
7. Though the worlds of all the Buddhas
    Are many as the Ganges' sands;
    Again, though there are numberless,
    Unenumerable regions,
    My splendour will shine everywhere
    And go throughout all these countries.
    My energy will be like this.

My magic power will be endless.
8. When I have become a Buddha
   May my country be the highest,
   Its people rare and excellent,
   Its field-of-Truth superlative,
   The land as good as Nirvāṇa,
   Matchless and incomparable.
   Then in pity and compassion
   I will liberate all beings.
9. Men from ten quarters who, reborn,
   Their hearts rejoicing and unstained,
   Have arrived inside my country
   Will dwell in peace and happiness.
   I call the Buddha to witness.
   He is my sincerity's proof.
   I have made my vows and in these
   Desires will labour earnestly.
10. The Buddhas of the ten quarters
    Are unobstructed in insight.
    May these Honoured Ones for ever
    Know what is done in my heart.
    Even though my body remains
    In the place of pain and poison
    I will walk in zeal and vigour,
    Patient, not regretting my vows.

11. THE SOLEMN OATH

The Larger Sukhāvatī-Vyūha Sūtra
Saṅghavarman's translation

After Dharmākara had made his forty-eight great vows, he recited the following stanzas.

1. My world-surpassing vow is established.
   I will surely reach supreme Buddhahood.
   Until these vows have been wholly fulfilled
   I swear not to become a full Buddha.
2. If during incalculable ages
   I am not a great lord of charity
   Everywhere saving the poor and distressed,
   I swear not to become a full Buddha.
3. When I have fully achieved Buddhahood
   My name will sound throughout the ten quarters.
   If there is any place it is not heard
   I swear not to become a full Buddha.
4. Free from lust, profound in meditation,
   Pure in insight, living the holy life
   And firmly seeking supreme Buddhahood,
   I will be the teacher of gods and men.
5. My magic force will generate great light
   Which will shine everywhere on boundless lands
   And dispel the three defilements' darkness
   And save all those in danger and distress.
6. I will open up the eye of wisdom
   And will destroy the darkness of the blind.
   I will stop up the evil destinies
   And open out the gates of good rebirth.

7. When my virtue is fully completed
   My sublime rays will light the ten quarters.
   Sun and moon will not release their radiance
   And the stars of heaven will be obscured.
8. I will open Truth's store to the people
   And give out virtue's treasures far and wide.
   Constantly among a great assembly
   I will preach the Law with a lion's roar.
9. I will offer worship to all Buddhas
   And be endowed with all roots of virtue.
   When my vows and insight are perfected
   I will be the hero of the three worlds.
10. Unobstructed wisdom like the Buddha's
    Pervades the universe and shines on all.
    May the strength of my merit and insight
    Be equal to this supreme Honoured One's.
11. If this vow is to achieve fruition
    The great thousand worlds will be moved and quake
    And all the gods up in the open sky
    Will rain down precious, exquisite blossoms.

12. MERCY AND THE VOID

The Laṅkāvatāra Sūtra, Chapter Two
Chinese translation by Śikṣānanda, A.D. 700-4

This scripture is a philosophical hold-all into which notes on the Void, Suchness, the eight consciousnesses, the three Bodies, and the bodhisattva course have all been crammed. It was influential during the formative period of Chinese Buddhism, and had an important part in shaping Zen thought.

1. The world is free from birth and destruction.
   It is like a flower blooming in the sky.
   In wisdom 'is' and 'is not' are absent,
   Yet the mind of great mercy awakens.
2. All the elements are like a phantom.
   They are far beyond mind and consciousness.
   In wisdom 'is' and 'is not' are absent,
   Yet the mind of great mercy awakens.
3. The world is eternally like a dream,
   Beyond eternalism and nihilism.
   In wisdom 'is' and 'is not' are absent,
   Yet the mind of great mercy awakens.
4. You know there is no self in men or things.
   The moral defilements and their burning
   Are always pure and without qualities.
   Yet your mind of great mercy awakens.
5. The Buddha does not dwell in Nirvāṇa.
   Nirvāṇa does not dwell in the Buddha.
   It transcends Awakening and Wakened,
   Transcends existence and non-existence.
6. The Essence Body, phantom-like, dream-like,

How can anyone recite its praises?
To know its no-nature and birthlessness,—
That is called reciting the Buddha's praise!
7. The Buddha has no marks of sense or sphere.
Not to see is called to see the Buddha.
How then can praises or defamation
Be uttered concerning the Holy One?
8. Those who see the Holy One as being
Tranquil, serene and far removed from birth,—
These men, in present and in after worlds,
Are free from attachment, grasping nothing.

13. IN PRAISE OF THE BUDDHA

Suvarṇaprabhāsa Sūtra, Chapter Twelve
Chinese translation by I-ching, A.D. 703

1. The countenance of the Buddha is like the clear full moon,
   Or again, like a thousand suns releasing their splendour.
   His eyes are pure, as large and as broad as a blue lotus.
   His teeth are white, even and close, as snowy as white jade.
2. The Buddha's virtues resembles the boundless great ocean.
   Infinite wonderful jewels are amassed within it.
   The calm, virtuous water of wisdom always fills it.
   Hundreds and thousands of supreme concentrations throng it.
3. The marks of the wheel beneath his feet are all elegant—
   The hub, the rim, and the thousand spokes which are all even.
   The webs [9] on his hands and his feet are splendid in all parts—
   He is fully endowed with markings like the king of geese.
4. The Buddha-body's radiance is like a golden mountain's;
   It is clear, pure, peculiar, without equal or likeness,
   And it too has the virtues of beauty and loftiness.
   Therefore I bow my head to the Buddha, king of mountains.
5. His marks and signs are as unfathomable as the sky,
   And they surpass a thousand suns releasing their splendour.
   All like a flame or a phantom are inconceivable.
   Thus I bow my head to him whose mind has no attachments.

14. THE AVATAMSAKA SŪTRA

Chinese translation by Buddhabhadra, A.D. 418–421

This voluminous scripture, which would fill a thousand-page encyclopaedia volume in complete English translations, covers the entire field of early Mahāyāna doctrine, but has the bodhisattva's course as a constant theme. A high proportion of the text is in verse.

Chapter Five

1. If a person thinks true enlightenment
   Is release, freedom from the influxes,
   And detachment from all things of the world,
   He does not possess the pure eye of truth.
2. If a person knows the Tathāgata,
   Discerning that nothing exists in him,
   And knows that all elements are extinct,
   That man will swiftly become a Buddha.
3. Whoever can look at this worldly realm
   In every aspect without attachment,
   And likewise the Tathāgata's body,
   This man will swiftly achieve Buddhahood.
4. If a person with overall sameness
   Conforms his mind to the Buddha-Doctrines
   And enters the non-dual doctrine's gate,
   That man is difficult for thought to judge.
5. If you perceive both self and Buddhahood
   As remaining in the sign of sameness,
   Then you will reside in no-residing
   And be far beyond all things that exist.
6. Form and sensation are without number;

     So are conception, thought and consciousness.
     He who understands well that that is so,
     That man is the great solitary saint.
7. If one understands all the elements—
    That nothing exists in the perceiver,
    That perceived elements are nothing, too—
    Then that one can illuminate the world.
8. Whoever perceives that all the Buddhas
    Appear in the world in the same instant
    And yet that nothing really arises,
    That person has a great reputation.
9. There is neither self nor living beings;
    Also there is no defeat and ruin.
    Whoever obtains such knowledge as this,
    Will accomplish supreme enlightenment.
10. In the one he understands the countless.
    In the countless he understand the one.
    Evolving lives are not reality.
    For the man who is wise there is no fear.

Chapter Thirteen

His heart of great kindness and compassion
Pervades the domains of the ten quarters.
He discerns all Buddhas' territories,
The Buddhas' Doctrines, and the three periods.
He wants to acquire the Buddha-virtues,
And the bodhisattva's truth-store ocean,
To help and benefit living beings.
Hence he first puts forth the thought of bodhi.
He wants to know everything in detail,—
The Realm of Essence, which resembles space,
All the kinds of ordinary beings,
All the Buddhas, and the Buddhas' Doctrines.

He wishes to obtain all the Buddhas'
Power of reaching and staying in all paths,
To arrive at the state of non-lapsing
And benefit ordinary beings.
Towards all the multitudes of beings
He ever arouses great compassion.
He keeps far away from thoughts of anger
And cultivates a benevolent heart.
His pity's light shines on the ten quarters
And makes a refuge for the multitudes.
All the Buddhas guard and remember him.
His excellence is inconceivable.
He wants to know everything in detail,—
The territories of all the Buddhas;
The Tathāgata's fine Essence Body
Whose profoundness is hard to imagine;
And the infinite store of excellence
Whose insight is extremely deep and vast.
Therefore his aspiration awakens
And he seeks Buddhahood with single aim.
He wants to know everything in detail,—
All the kinds of ordinary beings,—
And throughout the worlds of the ten quarters
To have unchecked, unobstructed insight.
In all the worldly realms, gross and subtle,
Or immeasurably narrow and broad,
Within everything he perceives the one,
And in the one he perceives everything.
The bodhisattva in those practices
Works earnestly and is not neglectful,
Not shunning pain, not clinging to pleasure,
Because he wants to save living beings.
He appears in front of all the Buddhas

And looks on them gladly, insatiably.
He enters all the profoundest doctrines,
The immeasurable seas of virtue.
All living beings upon the five paths
He cares for as he would an only child,
Cleansing them of many impurities
And endowing them with pure qualities.
He wants to make all seeds of Buddhahood
Accomplish their purpose and not perish.
He throws down and subdues all the Māras,
Destroying them, leaving none remaining.
He looks alike on the Tathāgatas
And the traits of all things in the three times.
The profound, subtle, marvellous Doctrine
He always cultivates diligently.
The bodhisattva always likes to look
On the dominions of all the Buddhas.
For this reason all the Tathāgatas
Baptize him with the nectar of insight.
The faith of his heart cannot be stopped up.
In steadfastness he is like a diamond.
In the presence of all Tathāgatas
He makes known his gratitude for their grace.
The highest, paramount domain, being
The immeasurable light of insight,
Awakens of itself, not through others.
The bodhisattva, when he first aspires,
Can understand everything in detail,—
The lusts of the five paths' living beings,
All kinds of action and retribution
And everything that is done by the mind.
He knows all senses' keenness or dullness,
Countless, innumerable characters,

And the domain which transcends everything.
The bodhisattva when he first aspires
Has endless desire for enlightenment,
Equal to the purest Realm of Essence,
Without attachment and without support,
As free from defilement as the ether.
He has accomplished a Buddha's insight;
His mind has no hindrance or obstruction;
He clearly knows the region of real truth;
He is in cessation, free from falsehood.

Chapter Twenty

Tathāgata does not enter the world,
And neither does he enter Nirvāṇa.
Through his original vow's great power
He manifests the self-existent Law.
This Law is difficult for thought to judge.
It is not in the domains of the mind.
Achieve the wisdom of the other shore.
Then you will see the realm of the Buddhas.
The form-body is not Tathāgata.
Similarly, sound is not him, either.
Yet, inseparable from form and sound
There is the Buddha's self-existent power.
Small wisdom is unable to perceive
The most profound domain of Buddhahood.
Accomplish knowledge of your past actions.
Then you will penetrate the Buddha's realm.
There is no place from which the Buddhas come.
Nor is there any place to which they go.
The pure and wonderful Essence Body
Manifests its self-dependent power.
Throughout innumerable worldly realms

It shows forth the Tathāgata's body,
Preaching widely the excellent Doctrine,
And in its mind there is no attachment.
The infinite, unlimited insight
Is unimpeded by the elements.
It enters the profoundest Realm of Essence
And displays its self-existent power.
Living beings and all the elements
It understands fully, unimpeded.
Its transformation bodies are countless,
Appearing everywhere in all regions.
If you wish to discover all-knowledge
And by yourself gain true enlightenment,
First you will have to purify your mind
And practise all the bodhisattva-acts.
This way you will see the Tathāgata's
Innumerable self-dependent powers,
Remove doubts for ever, and come near to
The paramount good friend and counsellor.

Chapter Twenty-two, Part Five

So in this way all the bodhisattvas
During the course of infinite ages
With earnest mind constantly cultivate
Each and every rudiment of goodness,
Worshipping innumerable Buddhas,
Solitary buddhas, and arahants,
In order to profit living beings.
Then they get the thought of enlightenment.
Diligently they keep the precepts' way,
With cleansings removing the filth of sin,
Developing the patience of goodness,
Filled with the grand virtue of contrition,

Through circumstances of merit and insight,
Their distance-conquering minds bright and pure,
Delighting deeply in Buddha-wisdom,
They rouse a Buddha-like (thought of) bodhi,
They offer worship to all the Buddhas
Of the ten quarters and the three periods.
Countries as endless as the sky itself
They wholly and utterly purify.
Since they understand well and entirely
The equalness of all the elements,
They put forth the thought of enlightenment
In order to save all living beings.
So in this way all the bodhisattvas
Produce this immeasurable thought,
And enter the STAGE OF REJOICING,
Cease evil, and delight in charity.
Attaining all powers of primal vows,
Amplifying the heart of compassion,
Walking thoroughly the ten paths of good,
They may arrive at IMMACULATE STAGE.
They complete the virtue of discipline,
Care for the world with a heart of kindness,
For ever keep free from all defilement,
And are constantly pure in the deep heart.
They consider all the worlds everywhere
As a raging fire of the three poisons.
The great heroes who act in this manner
Go into the third, the STAGE OF BRILLIANCE.
They observe that the three worlds are all void
And impermanent, and like a disease,
Like an ulcer, like a boil or arrow.
Countless sufferings blaze perpetually.
Seeing the faults of all conditioned things

They long gladly for the Buddha's virtue,
Obtain Buddha-wisdom's blazing brilliance,
And enter the fourth (BLAZING INSIGHT) STAGE.
They complete recollection and insight
And arrive at the wisdom of the Way.
During their stay in this land they worship
Hundreds of thousands of Tathāgatas.
They always meditate ably upon
The countless virtues of all the Buddhas.
They achieve their entry into the most
DIFFICULT-TO-ACHIEVE STAGE in the world.
Through the device of insight they can
Exhibit in many diverse manners
All possible forms of activity,
Thereby giving benefit to the world.
They offer worship to all the Buddhas
And do things that profit living beings.
Face to face with the unborn elements
They succeed in entering PRESENCE STAGE.
Even the whole world could hardly recount
All the bodhisattva's activities.
Thoughts of 'I' are ever absent from them.
They wholly avoid both 'is' and 'is not'.
From the first, elements are void and still,
Yet they function through the twelve causal links.
Understanding well this subtle wonder
They acquire entry to FAR-GOING STAGE.
Practising the skilful means of insight
They get the elements' extinctness sign,
And so, in this way, the bodhisattvas
Are hard to know and hard to emulate.
Because they wish to enable the world
To obtain good calmness and cessation,

They recommend the doing of all deeds
And many kinds of meritful conduct.
Everywhere they enter living beings'
Manifold places of mental action.
In this way they can gain entry to
IMMOVABLE STAGE, which is like the sky.
All the bodhisattvas with great wisdom
Can perform entirely and minutely
All the manifold actions of wisdom
And gain the ten self-dependent powers.
They are able through innumerable,
Infinite, incalculable bodies
To appear throughout the ten quarters' realms
And preach the wonderful Doctrine in them.
They ably penetrate the worldly realms
And the characters of living beings.
With this sort of great kindness and mercy
They can enter the STAGE OF GOOD INSIGHT.
The highest, wonderfully pure wisdom
Is able to perceive how all the world
Is enmeshed in the action of passions
And remains sunken deep in all hardships.
In order to liberate these people
They obtain the truth-store of the Buddhas
And preach well on the Highest Principle
Without the least distortion or error.
In this manner, proceeding in sequence,
They accomplish all the good qualities
Until now, when they have reached the ninth stage
And have developed merit and insight.
If you wish to gain the Buddhas' powers'
Highest, deep and wonderful benefit
And to receive the office of wisdom

Then in the presence of all the Buddhas,
First attain numberless concentrations
And extend your acts of wisdom vastly.
At last you gain the incorruptible
Exaltation, the seat of all wisdom.
If you are able to gain in this way
Increase of wisdom and exaltation,
You will be embellished with all treasures
When you come out of the royal lotus.
The bodhisattva matches the lotus
And shows his body seated upon it.
The bodhisattvas on the other flowers
All with a single mind look upon him.
At such a time the great bodhisattva
Emits from his body uncountable
Hundred thousands, myriad rays of splendour,
Extinguishing all the world's suffering.
And then from the crown of his head come out
A hundred thousand million splendid rays,
Shining through all realms of the ten quarters
On the great assemblies of all Buddhas.
In the middle of the sky overhead
The rays change into a net of splendour.
Having offered worship to all Buddhas
They go in underneath the Buddhas' feet.
Then at this time all the Tathāgatas
And also all the great heroes as well
Know that such and such a bodhisattva
Has been given the office of wisdom.
In the same way each and every Buddha
From between his brows emits splendid rays
Which are called ' the increase of all-knowledge '
And which enter this bodhisattva's head.

Each of the innumerable Buddhas
Confers office on this bodhisattva
Even as a wheel-revolving monarch
Confers his position on the crown prince.
Then worldly domains of the ten quarters
Are shaken throughout by a great tremor.
Right down to the Uninterrupted Hells,
All suffering is allayed and destroyed.
A bodhisattva, having accomplished
Every insight, succeeds to this office.
Such a one is said to have reached
The Truth-Cloud Stage, than which none is higher.

Chapter Thirty-four, Part Two

The unhindered body of great wisdom,
Being no body, is hard to conceive.
The Tathāgata's pure Essence Body
Cannot be fathomed by anybody.
His inconceivable activities
Have produced this immaculate body.
His countless wonderful embellishments
Suffer no defilement from the three worlds.
He illuminates all things everywhere,
And purifies all the realms of being.
He opens the gate of enlightenment
And produces deep absorption's wisdom.
He is ever free from all dirt and taint
And exterminates all the obstructions.
He is the brilliant pure sun of the world,
Everywhere releasing insight's splendour.
He has long cut off birth-and-death's current
And entirely purifies the three worlds.
He enjoys a bodhisattva's virtues

And has reached a Buddha's enlightenment.
He manifests innumerable forms
And no contamination is in them.
The multitude of forms he can display
Cannot be conceived by anybody.
The supreme insight of the king of men
Is able, in each and every instant,
To prepare infinite enlightenment.
Nobody is able to know it all.
He is endowed with infinite wisdom
Which is entirely indestructible,
And which within the space of one instant
Comprehends the Buddhas of the three times.
He discerns all actions separately.
With right thought he reflects on enlightenment.
Though he reflects, it is not reflection,
As the reflective elements are stilled.
Its profundity cannot be described;
It is far beyond the ways of language.
The Tathāgatas arise from this.
The Buddhas' acts are inconceivable.

15. AKṢOBHYA'S LAND

Mahāparinirvāṇa Sūtra, Chapter Twenty-two, Part One

This is a guide to rebirth in the paradise of Akṣobhya, the Buddha of the eastern quarter. There is a considerable literature dealing with this Buddha and paradise, though it is not a prominent theme in the *Mahāparinirvāṇa Sūtra*.

1. Do no injury to living beings,
   Hold firmly to all the rules of restraint,
   Accept the Buddha's exquisite teaching,
   And you will be born in Akṣobhya's Land.
2. Do not steal other people's property,
   Always be kind and generous to all,
   Everywhere build habitations for monks
   And you will be born in Akṣobhya's Land.
3. Do not ravish others' wives and daughters,
   Do not take your own wife at the wrong time,
   Have your bed in keeping with the precepts,
   And you will be born in Akṣobhya's Land.
4. Keep watch on your mouth and avoid false speech
   Either for your own sake or for others,
   In search of advantage or out of fear
   And you will be born in Akṣobhya's Land.
5. Do not slander any good acquaintance,
   Keep far away from evil company,
   Let your mouth always speak agreeably,
   And you will be born in Akṣobhya's Land.
6. Be the same as all the bodhisattvas,
   Always free from evil utterances,

      So that men will gladly hear what you say,
      And you will be born in Akṣobhya's Land.
7. Even when you are playing and laughing
    Do not utter inappropriate words,
    Be careful always to speak timely words,
    And you will be born in Akṣobhya's Land.
8. Seeing others receive gain and service,
    Let your thoughts be always those of gladness.
    Never let knots of jealousy be tied,
    And you will be born in Akṣobhya's Land.
9. Cause no affliction to living beings,
    Let your thoughts always be those of kindness,
    Do not employ evil expedients,
    And you will be born in Akṣobhya's Land.
10. Perverted views say there is no giving
     To one's parents, no past and no future.
     If you do not entertain such notions
     Then you will be born in Akṣobhya's Land.
11. Dig good wells beside roads in the desert,
     Plant and cultivate orchards of fruit trees,
     Always give nourishment to mendicants,
     And you will be born in Akṣobhya's Land.
12. If to the Buddha, Doctrine and Order
     You offer one incense lamp in worship
     Or even present a single flower,
     Then you will be born in Akṣobhya's Land.
13. If either because of apprehension
     Or for the sake of profit or merit
     You write out one stanza of this scripture
     Then you will be born in Akṣobhya's Land.
14. If, for the hope of profit and fortune
     In the course of one day you are able
     To read and recite this scriptural text,

Then you will be born in Akṣobhya's Land.
15. If, for the sake of supreme enlightenment
Throughout a whole day and throughout one night
You adhere to the eight rules of fasting,
Then you will be born in Akṣobhya's Land.
16. If you do not reside in the same place
As those who violate the chief precepts
And scold slanderers of the expanded texts,
Then you will be born in Akṣobhya's Land.
17. If you can give charity to the sick,
Even if it is just a piece of fruit
And giving them a pleasant, cheering glance,
Then you will be born in Akṣobhya's Land.
18. If you do not steal the Order's offerings
But guard the property of the Buddha
And paint and sweep Buddha and Order's sites,
Then you will be born in Akṣobhya's Land.
19. If you make images and Buddha-shrines,
Even if they are only a thumb's size,
And if you always take delight in them,
Then you will be born in Akṣobhya's Land.
20. If for the sake of this scriptural text
Your own body, your wealth and your treasures
You give to the preacher of the Doctrine,
Then you will be born in Akṣobhya's Land.
21. If you are able to listen, write down,
Receive, and remember and read and recite
All the Buddha's reservoir of secrets,
Then you will be born in Akṣobhya's Land.

16. THE TWELVE VERSES OF ADORATION

The Praises of Rebirth

by Shan Tao

1. I bow to him who is honoured by gods and men,
   Amida the deathless, the noblest being with two feet.
   He lives in his wonderful Land of Peace and Happiness
   Surrounded by a countless assembly of Buddha's sons.
2. His gold-coloured body is pure as the king of mountains.
   His still meditation proceeds like an elephant's tread.
   His two eyes are as pure as an azure lotus blossom.
   Thus I bow in worship to the Noble One, Amida.
3. His face is like the full moon in roundness and purity.
   His majestic light resembles a thousand suns and moons.
   His voice is like the drum of the gods and like nightingales.
   Thus I bow in worship to the Noble One, Amida.
4. He stands on the front of the crown Kwannon wears on his head.
   With all his excellent features and precious ornaments
   He subdues the arrogance of devils and outsiders.
   Thus I bow in worship to the Noble One, Amida.
5. Being incomparably pure and without defilement,
   The mass of his virtues is as glistening clear as the sky.
   He has attained self-dependence in conferring welfare.
   Thus I bow in worship to the Noble One, Amida.
6. Throughout the ten quarters, crowds of famous bodhisattvas
   And innumerable devils ceaselessly chant his praises.
   For all living beings the power of his vow is maintained.
   Thus I bow in worship to the Noble One, Amida.
7. A lotus flower grows in the gold-bottomed jewel pond,

An excellent high throne created by his root-of-goodness.
   Seated on this throne he resembles the king of mountains.
   Thus I bow in worship to the Noble One, Amida.
8. All the sons of the Buddha, coming from the ten quarters,
   Display their magic powers and arrive in Sukhāvatī,
   Gaze up at the Noble One's face and worship ceaselessly.
   Thus I bow in worship to the Noble One, Amida.
9. "All existing things are impermanent and without self.
   They are like the moon in water, lightning, shadows and dew."
   Without words he preaches this Doctrine to the assembly.
   Thus I bow in worship to the Noble One, Amida.
10. That Noble One's Buddha-field knows no mention of evil,
    Nor is there fear of female birth or evil destinies.
    All the people whole-heartedly worship that Noble One.
    Thus I bow in worship to the Noble One, Amida.
11. In that Noble One's countless regions of effective means
    There are no evil destinies or wicked counsellors.
    Those born there attain enlightenment without regression.
    Thus I bow in worship to the Noble One, Amida.
12. I have related the facts of that Noble One's virtues.
    His good qualities are boundless as the ocean's water.
    The roots of good and purity which I have thus acquired
    I transfer to living beings for birth in that country.

17. THE EVENING HYMN OF PRAISE

The Praises of Rebirth, by Shan-Tao
(adapted from *The Larger Sukhāvatī-Vyūha Sūtra*)

Praise! We most sincerely dedicate our lives in worship
To Amida Buddha of the Western Quarter.

1. The sea of Amida's wisdom and vow
   Is deep and broad, without shore or bottom.
   Those who hear his name and wish for rebirth
   Will each and every one reach his country.

May all living beings be reborn in the Land of Peace and Joy.

(*This refrain precedes and follows each verse.*)

2. The sixty-and-seven hundred billion
   Bodhisattvas who are beyond relapse
   That there are within this wordly domain
   Will each and all obtain birth in that land.
3. The bodhisattvas who are few in deeds
   And those who have developed scant merit,
   Whose number cannot be calculated,
   Will each and all obtain birth in that land.
4. The crowds of bodhisattvas and monks
   In the Buddha-fields of the ten quarters
   Could not be counted in an entire age.
   Each and all will obtain birth in that land.
5. Every one of all the bodhisattvas
   Each offers beautiful celestial flowers,
   Precious incense, and garments without price
   To serve and worship Amida Buddha.
6. Each one of them plays celestial music,

      Produces elegant, harmonious sound,
      Singing praise to the supreme Honoured One,
      Offering worship to Amida Buddha.

7. The sun of insight shines upon the world
   And melts away the clouds of birth-and-death.
   They walk three times around in reverence
   And bow to the Honoured One, Amida.

8. When they see that awe-inspiring Pure Land,
   Fine, marvellous, unimaginable,
   They arouse the highest aspiration:
   "We vow that our lands too shall be like this."

9. In response the Infinite Honoured One's
   Countenance shows forth a joyful smile.
   His mouth emits numberless rays of light
   Which shine throughout the ten quarters' countries.

10. Returning, the light circles his body
    Three times, and enters the crown of his head.
    All the multitudes of gods and people
    Leap and skip, and everyone rejoices.

11. The Brahma-voice is like a thunderclap;
    The eight sounds awaken lovely echoes.
    "I am acquainted with all the wishes
    Of the upright who come from ten quarters.

12. When you reach that resplendent pure country
    You will soon gain supernatural powers.
    You are certain to receive predictions
    From Amida, and become enlightened.

13. They fly by magic and go through all fields
    Worshipping a million Tathāgatas,
    Paying respect, rejoicing, then leaving,
    Returning to the Land of Peace and Joy.

14. If a man is without roots of goodness
    He will not get to hear the Buddha's name.

       The proud, the vicious and the indolent
       Find it hard to have faith in this doctrine.
15. Those who saw the Buddhas in former lives
    Are able to have faith in this matter,
    To hear in humble reverence and observe,
    And to dance and skip in great rejoicing.
16. Anyone who is able to hear that
    Appellation of Amida Buddha,
    And rejoices even for an instant
    Will be able to get birth in that land.
17. If a fire should fill the great thousand worlds,
    Pass straight through it to hear the Buddha's name.
    Let those who hear the name sing joyful praise.
    Each and all will obtain birth in that land.
18. Ten thousand years and the Three Jewels will cease.
    This scripture will endure a hundred years.
    In that time those who hear it an instant
    Will each and all obtain birth in that land.
19. A Buddha-age is very hard to find;
    Men with faith and insight are hard to meet;
    To find and hear the seldom-found Doctrine
    Is exceedingly difficult to do.
20. To have faith and to teach others the faith
    Is even harder than other hard things.
    To instruct everyone with great mercy
    Is truly to give thanks for Buddha's grace.
21. May compassion enfold and protect us.
    May the seeds of the truth grow and flourish.
    Both in this life and in the after-life
    May the Buddha for ever preserve us.

Praise! We most sincerely dedicate our lives in worship
To the Bodhisattva Kwannon of the Western Paradise.
May all living beings be reborn in the Land of Peace and Joy.

Praise ! We most sincerely dedicate our lives in worship
To the Bodhisattva Daiseishi of the Western Paradise.
May all living beings be reborn in the Land of Peace and Joy.
Praise ! We most sincerely dedicate our lives in worship
To the pure, great ocean-like assembly of bodhisattvas in the
  Western Paradise.
May all living beings be reborn in the Land of Peace and Joy.

18. THE HYMN OF RIGHT FAITH

By Shinran (A.D. 1173-1262)
Founder of the True Pure Land Sect in Japan

I take refuge in the Tathāgata of Endless Life! [10]
Adoration to his unimaginable light! [11]

While Dharmākara Bodhisattva [12] was an aspirant
In training under the Buddha Lokeśvararāja,
Perceiving the origin of all the Buddhas' Pure Lands,
And the good and evil of these lands and their men and gods,
He established the supreme and all-surpassing promise
And put forth the seldom-found tremendous resolution.
He meditated for five ages, selecting from them.
He vowed repeatedly 'The ten quarters will hear my name.'

Everywhere he emits eternal, unlimited light,
Unobstructed light, matchless light, the king of blazing lights,
The light of purity, the light of joy, the light of insight,
Uninterrupted, inconceivable and nameless light,
A light surpassing sun and moon, which lights up myriad lands.
All the crowds of living beings are favoured with this light.

To invoke the prime vow [13] is the act of those set-for-right.
The 'sincere and joyful believers' vow is the ground cause.
That they are equal to Buddhas and gain Great Nirvāṇa
Is because the 'sure to reach cessation' vow [14] is fulfilled.

The Tathāgata's reason for appearing in the world
Was just to preach the ocean of Amida's primal vow.

The seas of beings in these evil times of five decays
Ought to believe the truthful words of the Tathāgata.

If we arouse, though even once, a thought of love and joy,
Even with unsevered passions we will reach Nirvāṇa.
Common men, saints and blasphemers all enter equally
As all waters, entering the sea, acquire one taste.
The enfolding light of his heart ever shines to guard us.
Yet though ignorance's darkness is already shattered,
Still the mists and clouds of anger and of cupidity
Constantly obscure the sky of sincere and earnest faith,
Even as, although the bright sun is hidden by the clouds
It is no longer dark, but bright below the clouds and mists.
Have faith, listen reverently, and rejoice in the blessing,
And right away you will transcend the five bad destinies.
Each and all, both good and evil, common sinful people
If they hear and trust the Tathāgata's mighty promise,
The Buddha calls them great, supremely liberated ones.
The name for these people is 'puṇḍarīka lotuses'.

The Buddha-invocation of Amida's primal vow,—
For evil living beings in wrong views and in self-pride
Gladly to receive, trust and hold to this is hard indeed.
Among hard things there is no hard thing that surpasses this.

The philosophers of India, far in the western sky,
And noble monks in both the Middle Kingdom and Japan,
Showed that the Great Saint's real aim in coming into the world
Was to show how the primal oath responds to beings' needs.

Śākyamuni Tathāgata, on the Mount of Laṅkā,
Foretold to the assembly that in southern India
Nāgārjuna Bodhisattva would come into the world

To shatter all the theories of being and non-being,
To proclaim the supreme doctrine of the Great Vehicle,
To reach Joyful Stage and be born in Sukhāvatī.

He showed that the hard way is a painful journey on land,
And urged faith in the easy way, a pleasant trip at sea.
'If you call to mind Amida Buddha's primal promise,
Automatically, instantly, you enter certitude
And you only call the Tathāgata's name constantly
To give thanks as you should for the great oath's large compassion.'

Vasubandhu Bodhisattva, writing his treatise, said
"I take refuge in the Buddha of Unobstructed Light."
Relying on the sūtra he showed the Pure Land's real state.
He amply explained the great vow of abrupt transcending.
Leaning fully on the grace conferred through the prime vow's power
He explained single-heartedness to save common beings.
'If you turn and enter the great jewel-sea of virtue,
You are sure to gain entry to the Great Meeting's number.
When you reach the Treasury-of-Lotus-Blossoms Domain,
You will realize a true suchness and essence body
And travel through the woods of passion, showing magic powers,
Manifesting transformation in birth-and-death's gardens.'

Donran our teacher, towards whom the emperor of Liang
Always turned and offered rites as to a bodhisattva,
Learned the Pure Land doctrine from the scholar Bodhiruci,
Burned his Taoist books, and then took refuge in the Pure Land.
Commenting on Vasubandhu Bodhisattva's treatise,
He showed that the Reward Land's cause and fruit is the promise.

The grace for rebirth and return proceeds from other-power.
The source of deciding-for-right is just a mind of faith.
'If an ignorant, tainted common man arouses faith,
He will know that birth-and-death is the same as Nirvāṇa.
He will certainly attain the land of endless splendour.
And convert everywhere all living beings that exist.'

Doshaku settled that bodhi the saints' way was too hard
And made clear that only the Pure Land is enterable.
He deprecated the ten thousand good works of self-power
And urged exclusive calling of the perfect, virtuous name.
He kindly pointed out three marks of doubts and three of faith
As a merciful guide in the formal, last and dead Laws.[15]
'A lifelong evil doer, if he meets the vast promise,
Reaches the realm of peace and ease, attains the lovely fruit.'

Only *Zendo* clearly grasped what the Buddha really meant.
He pitied both the mindful and moral and the wicked,
And showed that the name is cause and the splendour condition.
'If he will enter the primal vow's great sea of wisdom,
Right away the disciple will receive the diamond mind.
After an instant of rejoicing and happy response,
Just like Vaidehi [16] he will acquire the threefold patience.
Thereafter he will know essence's constancy and bliss.'

Genshin, expounding widely the entire lifetime's teachings,
Leaned towards refuge in the Land of Peace and exhorted all.
Classing adherence as entire-deep and diverse-shallow,
He rightly distinguished the two lands of reward and change.
'The most sinful wicked man need only call the Buddha.
We also are within his encompassing protection.
Though our defilements blind our eyes, so we cannot see it,
Yet great compassion always shines unwearied upon us.'

Genku [17] my own teacher, who understood Buddhism clearly,
Had sympathy for good and evil ordinary men.
He set up the true religion in this remote island
And proclaimed the chosen primal vow in this evil age.
'If we return to wander in the house of birth-and-death
That which detains us is surely the sentiment of doubt.
If we would swiftly enter tranquil, unconditioned bliss,
A mind of faith certainly enables us to enter.'

The great sūtras' bodhisattvas and teachers of our sect
Have saved and rescued countless men from the gravest evils.
With the same heart people of this time, both monks and laymen,
Should simply have faith in the words of these eminent monks.

19. THE SŪTRA OF THE SIXTH PATRIARCH

Chapter Six

1. Deluded men cultivate merit rather than the Way,
   But they believe that cultivating merit is the Way.
   Though their merit from charity and worship is boundless,
   The three evils are originally done inside their hearts.
2. When you try to dissolve sin by cultivating merit
   You gain fortune in after-life, but the sin still remains.
   Just turn within your minds and remove sin's preconditions,
   And each in your self-nature perform the true repentance.
3. Suddenly wake to the Great Vehicle's true repentance,
   Get rid of wrong, practise right, and then you will have no sin.
   In learning the Way, always look into your self-nature,
   Since it is identical with that of all the Buddhas.
4. Our patriarchs only transmitted this abrupt doctrine,
   Wishing all to see their natures and share the one essence.
   If you wish hereafter to look at the Essence Body,
   Keep free from phenomenal marks and cleanse your inner mind.
5. Make an effort to see yourself; don't dissipate your thoughts.
   In later moments your life may be ended abruptly.
   If you wake to the Great Vehicle and can 'see nature',
   Join your palms devoutly and seek for it with utmost heart.

Chapter Ten

1. The self-nature of True Suchness is the real Buddha.
   The wrong views and the three poisons are the princely Māra.
   When you are wrong and astray, then Māra is in his House.
   When you have right vision, the Buddha is in his Temple.

2. Wrong views and the three poisons arising in your spirit
   Is the king Māra arriving to occupy his house.
   Right vision of itself clears the three poisons from the mind;
   Then Māra changes and becomes an authentic Buddha.
3. Essence Body, Enjoyment Body, Created Body,—
   The Three Bodies are fundamentally just one Body.
   If you turn within your nature and can see for yourself,
   You have ground for achieving Buddha-enlightenment.
4. At the root Pure Nature comes from the Created Body,
   And Pure Nature is always in the Created Body.
   This Nature makes the Created Body walk the Right Way
   Until it is fully rounded out and truly endless.
5. The lewd nature is basically the Pure Nature's cause.
   Remove the lewdness and it is the Pure Nature's body.
   Let everyone in his nature avoid the five lusts
   And in the instant he sees his nature it is Trueness.
6. If in the present life you meet the Sudden Doctrine School,
   You wake at once to Self-Nature and see the Honoured One.
   If you want by cultivating deeds to seek Buddhahood,
   You do not know the place in which you should search for Trueness.
7. If you can perceive Trueness for yourself inside your mind,
   Then that Trueness is your ground for becoming a Buddha.
   He who does not see Self-Nature and seeks Buddha outside
   Is an altogether ignorant man to have such thoughts.
8. The system of Sudden Teaching has now been left to you.
   To save the men of the world you must cultivate yourselves.
   I inform you who study the Way from this time onwards,
   If you do not have this vision you are wasting your time.

20. FAITH IN MIND

By Seng-Ts'an (died A.D. 606)

1. There's nothing hard in the real Way,
   But it declines to pick and choose.
   Simply be free from hate and love
   And illumination opens.
2. Given a hair's breadth of difference
   Heaven and earth stand far apart.
   If you would see it before you
   Do not concur, do not rebel.
3. Revolt and assent in conflict,—
   This is the disease of the mind.
   If you do not know the deep truth
   You strain in vain to still your mind.
4. Perfection resembles great space—
   Nothing short and nothing extra.
   Indeed, that you take and reject
   Is the reason you are not 'so'.
5. Do not chase outer connexions.
   Do not stay in empty patience.
   See all constantly as one kind
   And it will utterly vanish.
6. Stop motion to return to rest
   And rest is still in motion.
   If you stop in two-sidedness
   How will you know one-kindedness?
7. If one-kindedness is not known
   In two places merit is lost.
   Leave existence, you drown in it.

Follow the void, you turn from it.
8. The more words, the more reflection,
   The less you understand the Way.
   Cut off words, cut off reflection
   And you penetrate everywhere.
9. Turn to the root and get the truth.
   Follow semblance and lose the source.
   A moment turn from semblances
   And transcend the void before you.
10. Events in the void before you
    All spring from mistaken notions.
    It's useless to seek for the true.
    You must just quiet your notions.
11. Do not remain in the two views.
    Be careful not to pursue them.
    As soon as there is right and wrong
    Mind is lost in entanglements.
12. The two are because of the one.
    Do not hold to the one, either.
    If the one mind does not arise
    The ten thousand things are faultless.
13. Where there is no fault, no things are.
    Where nothing rises, no mind is.
    Subjects are quenched with their objects;
    Objects sink after their subjects.
14. Objects are objects through subjects;
    Subjects are subjects through objects.
    If you wish to know the two parts,
    At the source they are the one void.
15. The one void makes the two the same
    And holds the ten thousand forms alike.
    If it doesn't see fine and coarse
    How can there be taking sides?

16. The Great Way's style is liberal.
    It has nothing easy or hard.
    Small views hesitate and waver;
    The more their haste, the less their speed.
17. Cling to it, and you lose measure;
    You will surely enter wrong roads.
    Let it go, and it is itself;
    Its essence neither goes nor stays.
18. Trust nature, accord with the Way
    And be at ease, free from trouble.
    Bind your thoughts and they swerve from truth,
    Getting dull, sodden and unwell.
19. When unwell, you force your spirit.
    What use then are dislikes and likes?
    Would you mount the One Vehicle?
    Do not hate the six sense-objects.
20. If you don't hate the six objects
    You are as good as a Buddha.
    The wise man is free from action;
    The foolish man ties his own bonds.
21. In truth there are no different things.
    Ignorance makes its own clinging.
    To use mind to employ the mind,—
    Is this not the greatest mistake?
22. Error thinks of rest and trouble;
    The wakened have no likes or hates.
    Everything which is two-sided
    Springs indeed from reflective thought.
23. Visions in dreams, flowers in the air,—
    Why struggle to grasp hold of them?
    Getting and losing, right and wrong,—
    Leave them, get rid of them at once!
24. If an eye never falls asleep

All dreams will vanish of themselves.
If mind does not become varied
The myriad things are one suchness.
25. The real mystery of one suchness
Leaves affinities far below.
View the myriad things equally
And you come home to self-so-ness.
26. Put an end to the reason why
And analogies cease to be.
Stop motion, there is no motion;
Move stillness, there is no stillness.
Since the two are not complete
How should the one itself be so?
27. The frontier of the ultimate
Is not kept by laws and standards.
To fit mind's overall sameness
Still all performances alike.
28. When perplexities are cleaned out,
Right faith is attuned and straightened;
Nothing whatsoever remains;
There is nothing to remember.
29. It is void, bright, self-reflecting;
It does not labour the mind's force.
This place is not for thought's measure;
Cognition cannot fathom it.
30. In true nature's realm of being
There is neither other nor self.
If you would understand quickly,
We only say it is not-two.
31. In the not-two all is the same.
No thing is not contained in it.
The wise throughout the ten quarters
All enter this cardinal source.

32. The source neither hurries nor lags;
    One instant is ten thousand years.
    It is not present or absent
    But everywhere before our eyes.
33. The very small equals the large;
    For the sense-spheres are forgotten.
    The very large equals the small,
    For length and breadth do not pertain.
34. Existence is non-existence;
    Non-existence is existence.
    If anything is not this way
    You must surely not maintain it.
35. One is the same as everything;
    Everything is the same as one.
    If you can just realize this,
    Why worry about finishing?
36. Where faith in mind is the not-two
    And the not-two is faith in mind,
    Here the way of language ceases.
    It is not past, now or future.

BIBLIOGRAPHY

Edward Conze, *Buddhism, Its Essence and Development*. Bruno Cassirer (Publishers) Ltd., 1951.

Edward Conze (editor), *Buddhist Texts*. Bruno Cassirer (Publishers) Ltd., 1954.

F. Harold Smith, *The Buddhist Way of Life*. Hutchinson's University Library, 1951.

D. T. Suzuki, *Manual of Zen Buddhism*. Rider and Company, 1950.

E. J. Thomas, *The Perfection of Wisdom*. "The Wisdom of the East Series", 1951.

Wong Mou Lam (translator), *The Sutra of Wei Lang* (Hui Neng). Luzac and Company Ltd., 1947.

NOTES

1. 'Māyā' means 'magical illusion'. The name compares her to a beautiful maiden created by a magician.
2. Śākyamuni's two teachers, before he went his own way to enlightenment.
3. Five ascetics in whose company Śākyamuni had practised austerities. They deserted him when he gave up extreme forms of mortification.
4. At the Buddha's first sermon, the five ascetics and eighty thousand gods attained realization.
5. When Śākyamuni became a Buddha, the Buddha-Jewel appeared. When he first preached, the Doctrine-Jewel appeared. When the five ascetics were converted, the Order-Jewel appeared.
6. The eighteen special attributes of a Buddha.
7. A bird with a melodious voice said to be found in the valleys of the Himālayas. Its literary place is comparable to that of the nightingale in Western literature.
8. Gṛdhrakūṭa, a mountain near Rājagṛha, which is a favourite locale for Mahāyāna sūtras.
9. One of the signs of a Great Person is gauze-like webs on the hands and feet.
10. Sanskrit 'Amitāyus'.
11. A reference to 'Amitābha', which means 'Endless in Light'.
12. The bodhisattva who became the Buddha Amitābha when he finally reached enlightenment. It was customary for bodhisattvas to consider all the virtues of various pure lands, to choose those with which they wished to embellish their own pure lands, and to make the appropriate vows for achieving these virtues.
13. Dharmākara's eighteenth vow, the same as the 'sincere and joyful believers' vow, which is that all beings who with sincere faith and joy desire to be born in the Pure Land, and think this even seven times, will be born there.
14. Dharmākara's eleventh vow, that all beings in his land will remain in the group of those who are decided-for-right and will be certain to reach cessation and liberation.
15. The Dharma passes through four phases. After a Buddha, the True

Law prevails for five hundred years. In succeeding periods of five hundred years, follow the Counterfeit Law, the Final Law, and the Extinct Law.

16. Queen of Rājagṛha, and interlocutor in the Amitāyur-dhyāna Sūtra. See 'Sacred Books of the East', vol. xlix, p. 199.

17. Better known as Hōnen.

CHINESE REFERENCES FOR PASSAGES TRANSLATED IN THIS BOOK

References are to the number, volume, page and column of the *Taisho Issaikyo*

1. T. 192, IV.1.1, 2, 3 ; 28.1, 2, 3 ; 35.3 and 36.1, 2.
2. T. 210, IV.560.2, 3.
3. T. 201, IV.295.3.
4. T. 475, XIV.537.3 and 538.1.
5. T. 475, XIV.549.3 and 550.1, 2.
6. T. 352, XII.208.1 ; 209.2 ; 210.1 ; 210.1 ; 213.3 ; 214.1.
7. T. 262, IX.32.1, 2.
8. T. 262, IX.43.2, 3 and 44.1.
9. T. 262, IX.57.3 and 58.1, 2.
10. T. 360, XII.267.1, 2.
11. T. 360, XII.269.2, 3.
12. T. 672, XVI.590.1, 2.
13. T. 665, XVI.432.1.
14. T. 278, IX.422.3 and 423.1 ; 453.1, 2, 3 ; 485.3 ; 576.1, 2, 3 ; 682.2.
15. T. 375, XII.734.1, 2.
16. T. 1980, XLVII.442.1, 2, 3.
17. T. 1980, XLVII.441.1, 2, 3 and 442.1.
18. (Supplement) T. 2646, LXXXIII.600.1, 2, 3.
19. T. 2008, XLVIII.354.3 and 355.1 ; 362.1.
20. T. 2010, XLVIII.376.2, 3 and 377.1.

Other Titles of similar interest in The Wisdom of the East Series

THE ROAD TO NIRVAÑA. A Selection of the Buddhist Scriptures. Translated from the Pāli by E. J. THOMAS, M.A., D.Litt. "Contains familiar extracts from the Pāli scriptures with an excellent introduction covering the main points of the Buddhist belief."—*The Spectator.*

THE QUEST OF ENLIGHTENMENT. A Selection of the Buddhist Scriptures. Translated from the Sanskrit by E. J. THOMAS, M.A., D.Litt. "Every inquirer and advanced student will find here much of the greatest interest and real worth."—*Aryan Path.*

THE PERFECTION OF WISDOM. The Career of the Predestined Buddhas. Translated from the Sanskrit by E. J. THOMAS, M.A., D.Litt. "This delightful little book is a worthy addition to the Series. The reader is given a fine opportunity of learning at first hand what the scriptures say."—*Eastern World.*

KARMA AND REBIRTH. By T. CHRISTMAS HUMPHREYS.

THE SPIRIT OF ZEN. A Way of Life, Work and Art in the Far East. By ALAN W. WATTS.

POEMS OF CLOISTER AND JUNGLE. A Buddhist Anthology. By MRS. RHYS DAVIDS, M.A., D.Litt.

THE PATH OF LIGHT: Translated into English from the Bodhi-Charyāvatara of Sānti-Deva. A Manual of Mahayana Buddhism by L. D. BARNETT, M.A., Litt.D.

General Titles in
The Wisdom of the East Series

LITERATURES OF THE EAST : An Appreciation. Edited by ERIC B. CEADEL. With an Introduction by PROFESSOR A. J. ARBERRY, Litt.D. " This work is a valuable introduction to the great literatures of Asia."—*The Times Literary Supplement*.

EASTERN SCIENCE. An Outline of its Scope and Contribution. By. H. J. J. WINTER, Ph.D., M.Sc. " Dr. Winter has proved splendidly equal to the task ; a thoroughly satisfactory work."—*The Times*.

THE GLAD TIDINGS OF BAHA'U'LLAH. Extracts from the Sacred Writings of the Bahá'is, with an Introduction and Notes by GEORGE TOWNSHEND, M.A. " Enlightened and useful."—*Aryan Path*.

MANIFOLD UNITY. The Ancient World's Perception of the Divine Pattern of Harmony and Compassion. By COLLUM.

ONE IN ALL. An Anthology of Religion from the Sacred Scriptures of the Living Faiths. Compiled by EDITH B. SCHNAPPER, Ph.D. With an Introduction by BARON ERIK PALMSTIERNA. " A thoughtful and judicious selection."—*Aryan Path*.